Stories for Under-Fives

also edited by Sara and Stephen Corrin

IMAGINE THAT!: *Fifteen Fantastic Tales*
PET STORIES FOR CHILDREN
THE FABER BOOK OF CHRISTMAS STORIES
ROUND THE CHRISTMAS TREE
ONCE UPON A RHYME: *101 Poems for Young Children*
THE FABER BOOK OF MODERN FAIRY TALES
MORE STORIES FOR UNDER-FIVES
STORIES FOR FIVE-YEAR-OLDS
STORIES FOR SIX-YEAR-OLDS
STORIES FOR SEVEN-YEAR-OLDS
MORE STORIES FOR SEVEN-YEAR-OLDS
STORIES FOR EIGHT-YEAR-OLDS
STORIES FOR NINE-YEAR-OLDS
STORIES FOR TENS AND OVER
A TIME TO LAUGH: *Funny Stories for Children*
(Faber Paperback)
THE FABER BOOK OF FAVOURITE FAIRY TALES

retold by Sara and Stephen Corrin
Illustrated by Errol Le Cain
MRS FOX'S WEDDING
THE PIED PIPER OF HAMELIN

ff

STORIES FOR UNDER-FIVES

Edited by
Sara and Stephen Corrin

faber and faber

LONDON · BOSTON

First published in 1974 by Faber and Faber Ltd., 3
Queen Square, London WC1N 3AU. Reprinted 1975,
1978, 1981 and 1986. First paperback edition published
in the United States in 1989 by Faber and Faber, Inc., 50
Cross Street, Winchester, MA 01890.

Library of Congress Cataloging-in-Publication Data
Stories for under-fives / edited by Sara and Stephen
   Corrin.
   p.   cm.
   Summary: An anthology of modern stories and folk-
tales from England, Russia and Sweden, selected for pre-
school children.
   ISBN 057112920X $9.95
   1. Children's stories, 2. Tales. [1. Short stories. 2. Folk-
lore.] I Corrin, Sara. II. Corrin, Stephen.
PZ5.S88175   1989
[E] — dc 19   89-11966

Cover design by Janis Capone
Printed in the United States of America

Contents

———————————✳———————————

Contents

Contents

Acknowledgements

---------------------------------- * ----------------------------------

We are grateful to the undermentioned publishers, authors and agents for permission to include the following stories:

World's Work Ltd. and Harper and Row Inc. for *Little Bear Goes to the Moon* from *Little Bear* by Else Holmelund Minarik, and for *Big Sister and Little Sister* by Charlotte Zolotow.

World's Work Ltd. and William Morrow and Co., Inc. for *Miss Lollipop's Lion* by Judy Varga.

Longman Young Books Ltd. for *The Little Girl and the Tiny Doll* by Aingelda and Edward Ardizzone, copyright 1966; text from a picture storybook.

William Heinemann Ltd. for *Learning to Purr* from *The Wolf Who Was Sorry* by Ruth Ainsworth.

Hodder and Stoughton Children's Books (formerly Brockhampton Press Ltd) for *Mr. Fox* from *Folk Tales* by Leila Berg, and for *The Sick Cow* by H. E. Todd.

Anne English for *How the Animals Got Tails*.

Angus and Robertson (U.K.) Ltd. for *A Present for a Pig* by E. Watson, and *The Very Young Elephant* by Raymond F. Curtis, both from *Lucky Dip* edited by Claire Simpson.

Faber and Faber Ltd. and Houghton Mifflin Company for *Choo Choo: The Story of a Little Engine Who Ran Away* by Virginia Lee Burton.

Faber and Faber Ltd. for *The Little Wee Small Tiny Man* from

Acknowledgements

Nursery Tales by Diana Ross, and *The Little Armchair* from *Simple Tales for the Very Young* by Doris Rust.

Harvey Unna Ltd. and the author for *Little Laura on the River* by V. H. Drummond.

George G. Harrap and Co., Ltd. for *Teddy Robinson and the Band* by Joan Robinson.

Methuen and Co. Ltd. for *My Naughty Little Sister at the Party* by Dorothy Edwards.

Hilda Carson for *The Lion Who Couldn't Roar*, told on the BBC programme *Listen with Mother*.

The Elsa Beskow Estate for permission to translate the Swedish original of *Pelle's New Clothes* by Elsa Beskow.

A. M. Heath and Co. Ltd. for *The Cat Sat on the Mat* from *The Necklace of Raindrops* by Joan Aiken.

E. P. Dutton and Co., Inc. for *Monkey See, Monkey Do* by Inez Hogan, from the book *Monkey See, Monkey Do* by Inez Hogan, copyright 1960 by Inez Hogan.

The Bodley Head for *A Growing Tale* from *To Read and To Tell* by Norah Montgomerie.

Hutchinson Publishing Group Ltd. for *Mrs. Pepperpot and the Mechanical Doll* from *Little Old Mrs. Pepperpot* by Alf Proysen.

We should also like to thank Mary Junor, Schools Librarian, Barnet; Mrs. M. King and Carole Frances of the Hendon and Golders Green Children's Libraries respectively; Eileen Leach, Chief Librarian, Watford Junior Libraries; Mrs. S. Stonebridge, Principal Children's Librarian, Royal Borough of Kensington and Chelsea; Christine Jupp, Children's Librarian at Wall Hall College of Education; Mrs. D. Aubrey, Senior Children's Librarian, Borough of Wandsworth; Mrs. A. Foster, Children's Librarian; Winstanley Library, Wandsworth; Hazel Wilkinson, Senior Lecturer in Education at Wall Hall College; and, of course, Phyllis Hunt of Faber and Faber for her ever-ready advice and encouragement.

A Word to the Story-teller

---------------------------------*---------------------------------

Young children develop intense emotional associations with every situation and experience, and from these recurring associations a pattern of attitudes is built up which, even by the tender age of five, can be deeply entrenched. And so the child's earliest experience of stories—hearing them, sharing them, enjoying them—may well determine his attitudes to books and literature throughout life.

By the age of two the child begins to make-believe and he can already delight in his mother's most innocent fictions, such as the one about the little boy who finished his supper and got tucked into bed.

By the age of three and four fantasy takes over, and the line between real and fancy is indeed tenuous. The child plays without even needing to say "Let's pretend". He has his own rich inner fantasy life, in which Coleridge's "willing suspension of disbelief" happens spontaneously and he takes to stories as a duck to water. But he still has too little experience of reality; the frightening fantasy of magic and fairy-tale, which the slightly older child revels in, is not yet for him. The seven-year-old knows the fairy-tale is *not* true. ("It's very rare you get a true story nowadays," said one seven-year-old to us. "I used to believe in fairies but I don't any more; I do wish I still did," said another.)

A Word to the Story-teller

Stories for the very young must dwell on the reassuring and protective aspects; the escapades and adventures of the small creatures who people such tales as these always culminate in a return to safety. Choo Choo returns home a wiser and happier little engine.

Fear cannot be entirely eliminated. We know that the child in his own fantasy world grapples with fears which are sometimes terrifying; these must be aired and given expression. These stories will help children to resolve them; the emotional gratification and release of tension experienced when those who stray from safety survive narrow escapes and close shaves enable the child to work out his own difficulties and overcome feelings of littleness and inadequacy. He is, as Goethe says, "learning the eternal laws of life". Through these stories the child re-creates the world he knows, loves and understands, and a new world opens up to him.

These seemingly simple tales are full of action and suspense, with a clearly defined plot; and most of them contain those recurring refrains, those cumulative and repetitive elements, which children so delight in.

Stories are shared affairs and it will help, of course, if the teacher reads them in such a way as to convey her own enthusiasm for them. And this goes for the parent too, as well as for the uncle, aunt and elder sister. The teller should not shrink from adding a little trimming here and there to suit the capacity of the young listener. Above all, she must not fight shy of dramatising. All this is safely within the story-telling tradition; over the many years that tales have been handed down, they have been added to and embellished in all sorts of ways. But the basic themes remain.

Miss Lollipop's Lion

———————————————✳———————————————

Miss Lola Lollipop paced the floor in her kitchen. She was terribly worried. There was very little food in the house, practically no money, and she had a great many mouths to feed. Living with her were fourteen cats, nine dogs, three rabbits, seven canaries, four parakeets, two guinea pigs, and five hamsters, not to mention the donkey in the back yard.

Miss Lollipop couldn't look at a stray animal without bringing it home. She couldn't say "No," when someone asked, "Please give my pet a home—I can no longer keep it!" And homeless animals somehow knew they would find a place to stay if they came and sat on Miss Lollipop's doorstep.

Miss Lollipop sighed a big sigh and began to divide the little food she had among her pets. She gave each animal only a spoonful. Even so, there was hardly enough to go around. They all looked hungry and begged for more.

Just as she decided to give them her own supper as well, she heard a scratchy sort of noise at the front door.

"My, my," she said, as the noise grew louder, "it must be a homeless cat or dog. I'd better go and let it in."

Miss Lollipop opened the door and there, on her doorstep, sat, not a pussycat, not a dog, but a lion! The biggest lion Miss Lollipop had ever seen.

"Oh, do come in, you poor thing," said Miss Lollipop to the lion. "Welcome to the family." But to herself she said. "Whatever shall I do? Where shall I find the food this poor homeless lion will need?"

The lion padded into the parlour and spied six of the cats and five of the dogs. He pounced after them, knocking over furniture, vases, and whatever was in his way. He chased the cats, and he chased the dogs. He snarled at the parakeets and he roared at the hamsters. He put his big paw on one of the rabbits and held him fast. He let him go and caught him again, making terrible rumbling noises all the while.

"You stop that at once!" said Miss Lollipop, in a very strict voice. "Aren't you ashamed, teasing someone so much smaller than you?"

The lion looked very surprised and let the rabbit go. He lay down and did not move, not even when one of the pussycats started playing with the fringe on his tail.

"I'll give you something to eat after you've had a bath," said Miss Lollipop. "All pets who come to stay with me must have a bath. That's a rule of the house!"

She ran the bath water and fetched the scrubbing brush. "Come along now," she said to the lion. But the lion would not budge. He did not look as if he wanted a bath at all.

"No use arguing with me!" said Miss Lollipop. She pushed and pulled, and heaved and shoved, until she got the lion into the bath. The lion opened his mouth and showed all his big teeth. He growled, in a nasty sort of way. But Miss Lollipop paid no attention. She scrubbed and soaped and washed, as if she didn't hear him. She knew how to bring up pets the proper way. She wrapped the lion in a big towel and rubbed him dry. He smelled like rose-scented soap.

"I'd better do something about that messy-looking mane of yours. It is disgraceful," said Miss Lollipop. She combed out the

16

lion's mane and tied it with a pretty green ribbon on top, to keep the hair from falling in his eyes.

"Now you may stay in the parlour and play with the other pets, while I get you something to eat," said Miss Lollipop.

She searched the almost empty cupboard, but all she could find was her own supper—two sausages and a little leftover rice. She poured what milk she had left into a saucer and brought the food to the lion on a neat tray. The lion gobbled up the sausages and lapped up the milk. He turned his back on the rice and began to slink away.

"Finish your rice," said Miss Lollipop. "Finish it at once. We have no food to waste around here!" The lion ate the rice, every bit of it.

Miss Lollipop sat down in front of the fire. The lion lay down at her feet. He purred for a while and was soon fast asleep. But Miss Lollipop could not sleep. She sat all night in the armchair, trying to think of a way to earn some money, so she could buy food for all her pets and for the lion too. But she only knew how to care for animals and crochet antimacassars. And nobody wanted to buy antimacassars any more.

Early in the morning she played with all the pets to make them forget how hungry they were. She was teaching the lion a few tricks when she heard the doorbell.

I do hope it isn't someone with a new pet, thought Miss Lollipop. I simply can't take another one in!

There were five animal trainers and a fat man, who looked very upset, at the door. "We are looking for a fierce lion, who escaped from the circus last night. Have you seen him?" asked the animal trainers.

"No, I have not," said Miss Lollipop. "But a very nice lion came to my door, looking for a home. He is inside, playing. I've grown very fond of him already."

The fat man and the animal trainers rushed into Miss Lollipop's house. The lion stood in the parlour door. He began to roar.

"Quiet," said Miss Lollipop. "I can't hear my own voice!"

The lion sat down among the pussycats. He didn't roar, he didn't snarl, not even a little bit.

"Jumping catfish!" said the fat man. "That lion in your parlour, playing with your pussycats, is the fiercest lion in my circus, the one no one can tame. You wouldn't by any chance like a job as a lion tamer? I would pay you a lot of money!"

"What nonsense you talk," said Miss Lollipop. "Why he is the sweetest lion one could hope to meet. I'll come to work for you, though. I need money very much, and I never dreamed I could earn it in such an easy way!"

Miss Lola Lollipop became the most famous lion tamer ever. She never again had to worry about money, or how to feed her fourteen cats, nine dogs, three rabbits, seven canaries, four parakeets, two guinea pigs, five hamsters, the donkey in the back yard, and the twenty-seven new pets, who found their way to her doorstep. And sometimes, the lions came home to spend the weekend with her, because the lions loved Miss Lollipop and Miss Lollipop loved the lions.

Mrs. Rabbit's Cottage

———————————— ✳ ————————————

There was once a rabbit who had made herself a cosy little cottage out of the bark of an old oak tree. Not far away lived a fox who lived in a hut made of ice. The fox used to jeer at the rabbit. "Look," he would say, "my hut is all light but your cottage is dark and dismal."

Summer came and the fox's hut melted away. But the nights were still cool, so he went over to the rabbit's cottage and called out: "Mrs. Rabbit, may I come and share your cottage?"

"No, Mr. Fox," replied the rabbit.

"Mayn't I just stay in the yard outside?" he asked.

"No, Mr. Fox," said the rabbit. "You made fun of my cottage in the winter. Why should I be friendly with you now?"

Then the fox began to plead and beg until at last the rabbit let him into the yard. But no sooner was he in than he called out, "Mrs. Rabbit, please let me come and sit under your porch."

"No, Mr. Fox, you shall not," said the rabbit. "You shouldn't have jeered at me last winter.

So the fox pleaded and pleaded. "*Please*, Mrs. Rabbit, *do* let me sit under your porch," and at last the rabbit gave in. But no sooner was he seated under the porch than he said, "Please, Mrs. Rabbit, please let me come inside your cottage." "No indeed, Mr. Fox. No indeed I won't," replied the rabbit. "That I will not. You should not have made fun of my cottage last winter."

"Oh, please, kind Mrs. Rabbit, *do* let me come inside," pleaded the fox. And at last the rabbit let him in.

Inside it was all snug and cosy and the rabbit was sitting high up above the warm stove while the fox sat on a low bench.

The next day the fox said to the rabbit, "May I join you up there near the warm stove?"

"Most certainly you can *not*," said the rabbit. "You jeered at me last winter, didn't you? Besides, there's no room up here for two."

But the fox kept on begging and pleading and begging and pleading and so at last the rabbit allowed the fox to come and sit above the stove.

A day or two passed and the fox, if you please, started to push the rabbit out of the cottage! Of all the cheek! Yes, that is what he did. He started to push the rabbit out of her *own* cottage!

"Come on, out you get," said the fox roughly. "Out you get, you old squint-eye. I don't want to live here with you. There's not enough room." And he drove the poor old rabbit out.

Mrs. Rabbit's Cottage

And so the rabbit sat outside moaning and weeping.

By and by a dog came along.

"Why are you crying, Mrs. Rabbit?" he asked.

"Oh dear!" said the rabbit, "something terrible has happened. I had a nice cosy cottage made of bark. Mr. Fox begged me to let him come and live with me in my cottage. I did, but then he drove me out, yes, drove me out of my own cottage. Oh dear me, oh dear me!"

"Not to worry," said the dog. "I'll soon get rid of that fox for you."

The dog began to bark fiercely. "Out you get, Mr. Fox. Let Mrs. Rabbit back into her cottage, do you hear?"

The sly fox started to howl, pretending to be a wolf. "Aoul! Aoul!" he went. "If you dare to step in here or come any nearer, there'll soon be nothing left of you."

The dog was so scared that he scampered off with his tail between his legs.

The rabbit started weeping again. By and by a wolf came along and asked her. "What *is* the matter, Mrs. Rabbit? Why are you crying so bitterly?"

"Oh dear me, oh dear me!" said the rabbit. "Something terrible has happened. I had this nice cottage, all made of bark. I let Mr. Fox come in and share it with me and then he drove me out. Yes, he drove me out of my own cottage!"

"What a cheek!" said the wolf. "But never mind, I'll soon get him out."

So the wolf began to howl in the most fearsomely wolfish manner. "Come on! Out you get! At once, do you hear!" he said. The fox, very sly, pretended to be a tiger and roared back, "Clear out, you silly old wolf, or I'll devour you in less than a minute."

The wolf took fright at the tigerish roar and fled. And the rabbit once again started to weep.

Mrs. Rabbit's Cottage

By and by a cockerel came strutting along.

"Why on earth are you crying this fine day, Mrs. Rabbit?" he asked.

"Oh Mr. Cockerel, something terrible has happened to me," replied the rabbit. "I kindly allowed Mr. Fox to share my cosy bark cottage with me and he came in and drove me out. Yes, I tell you, drove me out of my own cottage! Oh dear me, oh dear me!"

"What a nerve!" said the cockerel. "But set your mind at rest, dear Mrs. Rabbit, I'll soon put an end to this nonsense."

"What, you?" asked the rabbit tearfully. "It's most kind of you to offer, I'm sure, but neither dog nor wolf could scare him away. So what could you do?"

"Just you wait and see," said the cockerel proudly.

He flew up to the topmost branch of a nearby tree, flapped his wings and crowed at the top of his voice: "Cock-a-doodle-do! Cock-a-doodle-do! Come this way, you fine hunters! This is where your prey is hiding—here, in this snug, bark cottage. The greedy, sly old fox is inside there. So come and shoot him out."

Mrs. Rabbit's Cottage

As soon as the fox heard the words "hunter" and "shoot", he was nearly frightened out of his skin. He rushed through the cottage door like a flash of red lightning and in two seconds he was out of sight. You may be sure, he was never seen anywhere near there again.

The rabbit was overjoyed. She invited the cockerel in to celebrate the defeat of the fox by making a most splendid dinner and she lived happily and safely in her cosy bark cottage for ever after.

The Little Girl and the Tiny Doll

———————————————— * ————————————————

There was once a tiny doll who belonged to a girl who did not care for dolls.

For a long time she lay forgotten in a mackintosh pocket until one rainy day when the girl was out shopping.

The girl was following her mother round a grocer's shop when she put her hand in her pocket and felt something hard.

She took it out and saw it was the doll. "Ugly old thing," she said and quickly put it back again, as she thought, into her pocket.

But, in fact, since she didn't want the doll, she dropped it unnoticed into the deep freeze among the frozen peas.

The tiny doll lay quite still for a long time, wondering what was to become of her. She felt so sad, partly because she did not like being called ugly and partly because she was lost.

It was very cold in the deep freeze and the tiny doll began to feel rather stiff, so she decided to walk about and have a good look at the place. The floor was crisp and white, just like frost on a winter's morning. There were many packets of peas piled one on top of the other. They seemed to her like great big buildings. The cracks between the piles were rather like narrow streets.

She walked one way and then the other, passing, not only packets of peas, but packets of sliced beans, spinach, broccoli and mixed vegetables. Then she turned a corner and found herself among beef rissoles and fish fingers. However, she did not stop but went on exploring until she came to boxes of strawberries; and then ice cream.

The strawberries reminded her of the time when she was lost once before among the strawberry plants in a garden. Then she sat all day in the sun smelling and eating strawberries.

Now she made herself as comfortable as possible among the boxes.

The only trouble was that people were continually taking boxes out to buy them and the shop people were always putting in new ones.

At times it was very frightening. Once she was nearly squashed by a box of fish fingers.

The tiny doll had no idea how long she spent in the deep freeze. Sometimes it seemed very quiet. This, she supposed, was when the shop was closed for the night.

She could not keep count of the days.

One day when she was busy eating ice cream out of a packet, she suddenly looked up and saw a little girl she had never seen before. The little girl was sorry for the tiny doll and wished she could take her home.

The doll looked so cold and lonely, but the girl did not dare to pick her up because she had been told not to touch things in the shop. However, she felt she must do something to help the doll and as soon as she got home she set to work to make her some warm clothes.

First of all, she made her a warm bonnet out of a piece of red flannel.

This was a nice and easy thing to start with.

After tea that day she asked her mother to help her cut out a coat from a piece of blue velvet.

She stitched away so hard that she had just time to finish it before she went to bed. It was very beautiful.

The next day her mother said they were going shopping, so the little girl put the coat and bonnet in an empty match box and tied it into a neat parcel with brown paper and string.

She held the parcel tightly in her hand as she walked along the street.

As soon as she reached the shop she ran straight to the deep freeze to look for the tiny doll.

At first she could not see her anywhere. Then, suddenly, she saw her, right at the back, playing with the peas. The tiny doll was throwing them into the air and hitting them with an ice cream spoon.

The little girl threw in the parcel and the doll at once started to untie it. She looked very pleased when she saw what was inside.

She tried on the coat, and it fitted. She tried on the bonnet and it fitted too.

She jumped up and down with excitement and waved to the little girl to say thank you.

She felt so much much better in warm clothes and it made her feel happy to think that somebody cared for her.

Then she had an idea. She made the match box into a bed and pretended that the brown paper was a great big blanket. With a string she wove a mat to go beside the bed.

At last she settled down in the match box, wrapped herself in the brown paper blanket and went to sleep.

She had a long, long sleep because she was very tired and, when she woke up, she found that the little girl had been back again and had left another parcel. This time it contained a yellow scarf.

Now the little girl came back to the shop every day and each time she brought something new for the tiny doll. She made her a sweater, a petticoat, knickers with tiny frills, and gave her a little bit of a looking-glass to see herself in.

She also gave her some red tights which belonged to one of her own dolls to see if they would fit. They fitted perfectly.

At last the tiny doll was beautifully dressed and looked quite cheerful, but still nobody except the little girl ever noticed her.

"Couldn't we ask someone about the doll?" the little girl asked her mother. "I would love to take her home to play with."

The mother said she would ask the lady at the cash desk when they went to pay for their shopping.

"Do you know about the doll in the deep freeze?"

"No indeed," the lady replied. "There are no dolls in this shop."

"Oh yes there are," said the little girl and her mother, both at once. So the lady from the cash desk, the little girl and her mother all marched off to have a look. And there, sure enough, was the tiny doll down among the frozen peas.

"It's not much of a life for a doll in there," said the shop lady, picking up the doll and giving it to the little girl. "You had better take her home where she will be out of mischief."

Having said this, she marched back to her desk with rather a haughty expression.

The little girl took the tiny doll home, where she lived for many happy years in a beautiful doll's house. The little girl played with her a great deal, but best of all she liked the company of the other dolls. They all loved to listen to her adventures in the deep freeze.

Learning to Purr

———————————— ✳ ————————————

One morning, when the kittens had lived with Mrs. Polly for a week, Tip woke up and said sleepily to Pansy, "Do you remember the nice purring noise mother used to make sometimes?"

"Yes, I do," said Pansy. "When she was pleased with us."

"Or sorry for us."

"Or wanted us to go to sleep."

"I wish I could make it," sighed Tip, "but I can't. I'll try again."

He did his best, but only made a choking sound, as though a fish bone were tickling his throat.

"Now I'll try," said Pansy, and she did her best too. "Is that right?"

"No," said Tip. "No, it's quite wrong. You sound as if you were ill. Mother always sounded peaceful and happy."

During the morning, a large, furry bumble-bee flew in through the kitchen window. He buzzed up and down the pane, trying to find a way out.

"Listen!" said Pansy. "He is almost purring. Let's ask him how he does it."

She climbed on to a chair and then on to the table and reached out a paw.

"Tell me how to purr, please," she asked.

Learning to Purr

"Purr indeed!" replied the bumble-bee crossly. "What rubbish you talk! I don't PURR! I BUZZ like all proper bumble-bees. I BUZZ with my wings. You have no wings, you poor creature, so of course you can't buzz."

Just then he found the part of the window that was open and he sailed out into the sunshine.

"Never mind," said Tip. "He was a cross fellow even if he did have wings. Listen—I can hear something else purring."

Pansy listened and she too heard a gentle, sleepy kind of noise. It was coming from the kettle on the stove.

Tip went as close to the hot stove as he dared and asked politely: "Kettle on the fire, can you tell me how to purr?"

"I would if I could," answered the kettle kindly, "but I am not purring. I am singing. I always start to sing just when the water inside me is ready to boil. Then Mrs. Polly lifts me off the stove before I splutter and boil over."

Just then Mrs. Polly came in, and sure enough she moved the kettle to the side, away from the hot flames. Then she went to the brush cupboard and took out the vacuum-cleaner. She plugged it into the proper place and began to sweep the rug. The vacuum-cleaner made a loud, whirring noise as it sucked up the dust.

Both kittens pricked their ears. Something was purring very loudly indeed. The floor seemed to tremble. They crept under the table and watched the vacuum-cleaner going up and down across the rug, purring furiously.

Mrs. Polly turned the switch off for a moment and the noise stopped. The kittens asked eagerly: "Will you teach us how to purr, please? We don't need to purr loudly like you. Quite a small, gentle purr would do."

"I can't teach you how to purr," roared the vacuum-cleaner as Mrs. Polly switched him on again. "You have to have a special dust-bag inside you, and special machinery. Could you ever learn to eat dust like I do? Sometimes I eat pins as well, and match-sticks and hairs and bits of coal. How would you like that?"

"We prefer milk and fish, thank you," said the kittens, and they crept back into their box.

"Don't let's worry about purring," said Tip. "It must be very difficult. I shall try to catch the end of my tail instead." He spun round and round like a top, but of course his tail spun round and round too, and he never quite managed to catch it. But it was fun all the same. When he stopped spinning round he was so dizzy that the room went on turning in a crazy way.

Learning to Purr

That evening, when it was time to go to bed, Mrs. Polly laid her knitting on the table and took the kittens on her lap for a cuddle before they went to sleep. She stroked them with her warm hands and tickled them gently under their fluffy chins.

"I can hear someone purring," said Tip sleepily.

"So can I," agreed Pansy. "Such a soft purr. Who can it be?"

"I don't know. I'm too sleepy to care."

"It's YOU purring," said Pansy.

"No, it must be YOU," said Tip.

They both listened again.

"Why, it's BOTH of us!" And so it was. They were so warm and sleepy and happy that they were purring without even trying.

Mr. Fox

———————————————*———————————————

Now this is the tale of a fox
and all the things that went into his bag.
And this is the way I tell it.

One day Mr. Fox was digging by his tree when he found a big fat bumble-bee. So he put it in his bag.

Then he walked, and he walked, and he walked, till he came to a house. And in the house there was a little black woman sweeping the floor.

"Good morning," said Mr. Fox.

"Good morning," said the little black woman.

"May I leave my bag here? I want to go to Squantum's house?"

"Yes, certainly."

"Very well then," said Mr. Fox. "But mind you don't look in my bag."

"Oh, I won't," said the little black woman.

So off went Mr. Fox, trot, trot, trot-trot-trot, to Squantum's house.

As soon as he was gone, I'm afraid the little black woman *did* look in the bag. She just peeped in. And out flew the big fat bumble-bee! And the little black woman's cock-a-doodle-doo ran and gobbled him up.

Mr. Fox

Presently back came Mr. Fox. He looked at his bag and he said, "Where is my big fat bumble-bee?"

And the little black woman said, "I'm dreadfully sorry, but I'm afraid I did look in your bag, and the big fat bumble-bee flew out, and my cock-a-doodle-doo gobbled him up."

"Oh really!" said Mr. Fox. "Then I shall take your cock-a-doodle-doo instead."

And he took the little black woman's cock-a-doodle-doo and put that in the bag instead. Then off he went.

He walked, and he walked, and he walked, until he came to a house. And in this house there was a little red woman darning socks.

"Good morning," said Mr. Fox.

"Oh, good morning," said the little red woman.

"May I leave my bag here while I go to Squintum's house?"

"Yes, certainly," said the little red woman.

"Very well then," said Mr. Fox. "But mind you don't look in my bag."

"I won't," said the little red woman.

So off went Mr. Fox, trot, trot, trot-trot-trot, to Squintum's house.

As soon as he was gone, I'm afraid the little red woman *did* look in the bag. She just peeped in, and out flew the cock-a-doodle-doo. And the little red woman's pig chased him down the lane.

Mr. Fox

Presently back came Mr. Fox. He looked at his bag, and he said, "Oho! Where is my cock-a-doodle-doo?"

And the little red woman said, "I'm very sorry, but I did open your bag. And your cock-a-doodle-doo flew out, and my pig chased him down the lane."

"Very well," said Mr. Fox. "I shall take your pig instead." And he put the little red woman's pig in the bag.

Then off he went. He walked, and he walked, and he walked, till he came to a house. And in this house there was a little yellow woman washing the dishes.

"Good morning," said Mr. Fox.

"Oh, good morning," said the little yellow woman.

"May I leave my bag here while I go to Squeeentum's house?"

"Yes, certainly."

"Very well then. But mind you don't look in my bag."

"No, I won't," said the little yellow woman.

Then off went Mr. Fox, trot, trot, trot-trot-trot, to Squeeentum's house.

As soon as he was gone, the little yellow woman *did* look in the bag. She just peeped in, and out jumped the pig. And the little yellow woman's little boy took a stick and chased him right out of the house.

Pretty soon, back came Mr. Fox. He looked at his bag and he said, "Dear me. Where is my pig?"

Mr. Fox

And the little yellow woman said, "I'm frightfully sorry, but I'm afraid I did look in your bag. And the pig jumped out, and my little boy took a stick and chased him right out of the house."

"My goodness," said Mr. Fox. "Then I shall have to take your little boy instead." And he took the little yellow woman's little boy, and put him in the bag.

Then he walked, and he walked, and he walked, until he came to a house. And in this house there was a little white woman making gingerbread. At one side of her sat four little girls. And on the other side sat a big black dog.

"Good morning," said Mr. Fox.

"Good morning," said the little white woman.

"May I leave my bag here while I go to Squoooontum's house?"

"Yes, certainly."

"Very well then. But mind you don't look in my bag." Then off went Mr. Fox, trot, trot, trot-trot-trot, to Squoooontum's house.

Now as soon as he was gone, the lovely smell of the gingerbread came out of the oven, and it smelled so good, so good that all the four little girls called out, "Oh, Mummy, Mummy, may we have some gingerbread?" And the little boy in the bag called out, "Oh, Auntie, Auntie, may I have some gingerbread?"

Well, of course, as soon as the little white woman heard a little boy calling out of the bag, she undid the bag at once. And out jumped the little boy. And so that Mr. Fox wouldn't notice anything, the little white woman put the big black dog in the bag instead.

Presently, back came Mr. Fox. He looked at the bag, and it still looked all bumpy and knobbly. So he thought it was just the same as before. He picked it up and off he went.

He walked, and he walked, and he walked, till he came to a good place to sit down. Then he sat down. And he untied the bag. And out jumped the big black dog. He was so hungry, because he hadn't had any gingerbread yet, that he gobbled up Mr. Fox completely.

And back in the little house, the little white woman took the gingerbread out of the oven. And the four little girls and the one little boy sat down at the table and they ate it all up. Except for one piece that they saved for their mummy because she baked it, and one piece that they gave to the dog when he came home, for eating up Mr. Fox.

How the Animals Got Tails

───────────────── * ─────────────────

There once was a time when none of the animals in the world had tails—not a single one. The horse had no tail to swish away the flies. The dog had no tail to wag when he was happy. And the monkey had no tail to curl round the branches when he was jumping from tree to tree.

The wise lion, who was King of the animals, knew there was something missing, and he thought and thought until he had a clever idea. "Animals. Animals," he roared, "I, the lion, the King of all the animals, command you to come to a meeting in the Great Meadow. Roar, roar!"

When they heard the lion roar every animal from far and near came hurrying to the Great Meadow. First came the fox and the squirrel, then the horse, the dog and the cat. Then came the monkey and the mouse. The lion waited for them all to arrive. "Sit in a circle round me," he told them, "and hear what I have to say." More and more animals came until the circle was almost complete. The elephant and the pig were nearly late, but last of all was the rabbit. He had been eating a carrot when he heard the lion roar, and had finished it before coming to the Great Meadow. And now he was the very last to arrive.

The lion held up his paw for silence. "Friends," he said, "I have been thinking." He paused. "I have been thinking that something is missing for all of us, so I have invented—TAILS."

How the Animals Got Tails

And he held up a huge bag full of tails.

"You will get one each," he told the animals "and wear your own always." How the animals clapped and cheered their clever leader. "Now, first come, first served," said the lion, "and as I was here first I get the first tail." And from the bag he pulled a marvellous long golden tail with a black tassel at the end, and put it on himself. How wonderful it made him look. He waved it proudly, while the animals watched, and waited for their tails.

The lion stood in the circle and called out, "The fox". He gave the fox a long, thick bushy tail, like a brush. Fox put it on and went away proudly.

"Next, the squirrel," said the lion. And the squirrel too got a huge bushy tail, which he curved up over his back before leaping away. The horse came next, and from the bag the lion

pulled a long, strong, black tail, combed out until it was silky and straight. The horse was delighted, and galloped off swishing his new tail from side to side.

How the Animals Got Tails

The cat and the dog came into the circle together, and they each received a straight tail, which would wave or wag from

side to side, or up and down, as they pleased. The monkey was given an extremely long tail. He curled it over his arm, so that he wouldn't trip over it, and went jumping away into the trees.

By now the bag of tails was half empty, so there was not much choice for the elephant when he came in his turn. In fact his tail looks like a piece of chewed string—just look at it, if you see an elephant. But he put it on quite happily, and lumbered off.

"Mouse," called the lion, and the mouse came. Now considering how small a mouse is, he did very well, for the tail pulled from the bag for him was very long indeed. Mouse put it on and scuttled away, trailing his tail behind him.

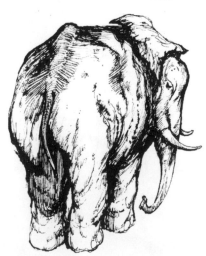 

How the Animals Got Tails

"Humph!" said the lion, as the pig came up. "Not much left now," and he took out yet another straight, stringy tail. The pig was not pleased. "The elephant and the mouse have tails like that," he said. "Can I have something different, please?" The lion shook his head. "Sorry," he said, "you arrived almost last, and this is all there is." "Oh, very well then," said the pig, taking the stringy tail and looking at it crossly.

"This will just not suit me," he muttered. "Just imagine a pig with a straight tail!" As he walked away he trod on a thick twig. "Hoink, hoink," he grunted, "I have an idea. Lions aren't the only ones with brains." And he took his tail and wrapped it tightly round the twig. When he pulled the twig out the tail stayed curly. "I like that better," pig said, and he stuck on his new curly tail.

Last of all to receive a tail was the rabbit. By now the lion was rather tired of tails, and he hurriedly shook the bag upside down to get out the last one. It was tiny—just a tiny thin piece of tail. Poor rabbit was disappointed, but he knew there was nothing else, so he thanked the lion and took the tail. But it was so small he couldn't bring himself to put it on.

"This is just a nothing tail," he told himself. "Not a bushy tail, like the fox's, or swishy like the horse's. Not even long enough to wave or wag. I will look silly with this one." He sighed. The lion had given them all tails, and they would have to wear them, rabbit knew.

As the rabbit wandered along, thinking about his piece of tail, he came to a prickly bush, and *he* had a wonderful idea. "Rabbits can think as well as lions and pigs," he said. And he took his tail and stroked it gently backwards and forwards over the prickles, until the tail became soft and round. "That's better," thought rabbit, looking at it happily. Then he stuck on his new fluffy tail, and bobbed away merrily.

A Present for a Pig

---------------------------------*---------------------------------

O ne morning when Sally woke up she felt very lonely. She was lonely because the day before, Tim, her brother, had gone away to school.

Although she had seven dolls, two teddy bears, and a whole shelf full of books, she still felt very lonely; she wished Tim were there to play with her.

Sally lived in the country, in an old farmhouse all built of stone. The house was on the side of a hill, and at the bottom of the hill was a road.

It was a long way up the road to the nearest town, and it was a long way down the road to the nearest house.

After breakfast, because she had nothing else to do, Sally walked down to the gate to meet Mr. Thomas. Mr. Thomas drove the baker's van, and as well as bringing the bread, he always brought the mail. It wasn't very long before she saw the van coming along the road, and by the time she had opened the gate Mr. Thomas had pulled to a stop.

"Three loaves of bread for you today," said Mr. Thomas, "and here are two letters, four newspapers, and . . . THIS."

THIS was an enormous parcel, all wrapped up in thick brown paper with lots of string, and a row of stamps. Sally held up her arms and Mr. Thomas piled the things on to them. They were piled so high Sally could only just see over the top, and she nearly tripped twice going up the path.

Mummy's eyes opened wide when she saw the parcel.

"Why . . . it's for you," she said.

You can imagine Sally's surprise when she heard this.

Off came the string! Off came the brown paper! Off came the lid of the box, and inside was a FAT PINK PIG. He had turned-over ears, a large snout, and his arms stuck straight out each side. He was dressed in a lovely blue-checked open neck shirt, and a pair of blue shorts with straps over the shoulders which did up in the front with two shiny white buttons. Pinned to his shirt was a note. It said:

Dear Sally,

I thought you might feel lonely now that Tim has gone away to school, so I have sent Pig to keep you company and cheer you up.

Love
Granny

A Present for a Pig

"He has certainly got a cheerful face," said Mummy, "and he certainly does look a very friendly Pig."

Sally thought so too, and she felt much happier.

Later, when she went to feed the hens, she propped Pig up on the fence so that he could watch her. Later still, when she had her lunch, Pig even sat up to the table. In fact, everywhere that Sally went, Pig went too. When bed time came, Sally put Pig in the bed beside her. Now Pig was very big, and because his arms stuck straight out each side of him there wasn't much room left for Sally.

That night when it was very dark, and everyone was fast asleep Sally must have stretched . . . or perhaps she tried to turn over, but, whatever she did, she didn't have any room to do it in, and with an AWFUL THUD she fell right out of bed on to the floor. Poor Sally, it did give her a fright!

Mummy and Daddy came rushing in to see what all the noise was about. They were amazed to see Sally on the floor. But it didn't take long to tuck her into bed again.

The very next night the same thing happened. And the next night, and the next.

The fifth night, Mummy was quite cross.

"You'll have to sit Pig on the floor," she said, "you just haven't got enough room." And she took him out and sat him by the bed.

But Sally thought Pig looked very sad sitting there in the cold all by himself. As soon as her mother had shut the door, she picked him up and put him back in the bed beside her. She was so determined that she wouldn't fall out of bed again, that she kept her eyes wide open all night long . . . she didn't sleep a wink.

The next morning, when Sally went out into the garden, she heard a lot of thumping and bumping, hammering and sawing. It was Daddy working in the barn. With Pig firmly tucked

47

under her arm, Sally went to watch him. But wherever she stood, she seemed to be in the way.

At last Daddy said, "I'm busy, Sally, you run along outside and play."

So she went into the kitchen. Her mother was cutting out some material. She had scissors, and pins, and reels of cotton everywhere.

"I'm busy, Sally," she said, "out you go and play."

So Sally and Pig went out and sat in the sun on the lawn where the daisies grew.

"I'll make you a daisy chain," Sally said to Pig.

First she made one for Pig and put it around his neck, then she made one for herself and put it around her own neck.

Then they sat together on the swing . . . and swung.

After tea that night Daddy came in with a parcel. It was so big he had wrapped it all around with sheets of newspaper.

"This," he said, as he carefully put it down, "is a PRESENT FOR PIG."

Sally tore off the newspaper, and there inside was the dearest little bed. It was just like her own with a top and a bottom, a wire, and it even had a mattress studded with buttons. Then Mummy brought her two blankets, two sheets, and a pillow.

That night, when Sally tucked Pig into his bed, he looked very very comfortable and happy.

Then Mummy tucked Sally into her bed, and kissed her goodnight and she

48

looked very comfortable and happy too. And, do you know, after that Sally never fell out of bed again.

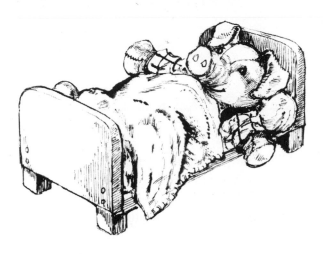

Farmer Giles's Goats

---*---

Farmer Giles had two fields. In one he grew some very nice turnips and in the other he kept his three goats—and very mischievous little goats they were.

One day the naughty goats ran out of their shed and into the turnip field. Farmer Giles was very cross but as he was too busy to see to the matter himself he sent his little boy. "Just run into the turnip field, son," he said, "and drive those three naughty goats out at once."

Farmer Giles's Goats

Off ran the little boy to try and chase the goats out of the field. "Shoo, shoo, out you get, you naughty goats," he cried, but they took not the slightest notice. The little boy was soon gasping for breath and went and sat down by the gate and cried.

Soon a horse came along. "Why are you crying, boy?" asked the horse.

"Because I can't drive the goats out of my father's turnip-field," cried the lad.

"Is that all?" asked the horse. "I'll soon settle that for you." And he galloped into the turnip-field crying, "Out, out, you naughty goats," chasing them for all he was worth. But the goats simply ran away to the opposite end of the field. The horse was soon out of breath and went and sat down beside young Giles and, like him, began to cry. So now there were two of them boo-hooing; and the naughty goats carried on eating Farmer Giles's turnips.

Soon a cow came along. "Why are you two crying, may I be so bold to ask?" asked the cow.

"Because we can't drive Farmer Giles's goats out of his turnip-field," they howled.

"Don't worry, my friends, I'll soon see to that," said the cow and she lumbered out into the field.

"Moo, moo, out you get, you naughty goats," she cried. But the goats ran much too fast for her and she was soon out of breath and gave up the chase. She, too, came panting over to young Giles and the horse and sat down and began to cry. So now there were three of them boo-hooing and boo-hooing. And the goats went on enjoying the turnips.

Next came a pig.

"And why, may I ask, are you lot crying your eyes out?" he queried.

"Because we can't drive the goats out of Farmer Giles's turnip-field," they wailed.

"Oho," said the pig. "I'll soon put that right." And off he trotted.

"Umph, grunt, humph, grunt, you naughty goats. Get out of this field, this very minute, d'you hear!" he squealed.

But the goats didn't pay much attention to him. They ran to the opposite corner of the field and soon the pig, gasping for breath, gave up and came and sat down by young Giles, the horse and the cow. And now there were four of them, all boo-hooing their hearts out. The naughty goats, of course, just went on eating the farmer's turnips.

After a while a bee came buzzing along.

"What's the matter with you four, then?" he asked. "I could hear you crying from miles away."

"It's because we can't drive the goats out of Farmer Giles's turnip field," they moaned.

"Not to worry," buzzed the bee, "I'll have them out in a jiffy."

The four of them stopped crying and stared in amazement at the bee.

"You could never do that," they said, "you're far too small." And they all burst out laughing.

"Just you wait," said the bee breezily and off he flew into the turnip field. He came down low above the goats, soaring above their heads and buzzing away for all he was worth.

"Bzzzz! Bzzzz! Bzzzz!" he went. "If you goats don't clear out of this turnip-field this very minute I shall fly down and sting the lot of you."

At this the three naughty goats galloped off as fast as their legs could carry them and never came back to the turnip-field again.

Young Giles, the horse, the cow and the pig were delighted. They thanked the bee and said, "My, what a clever little bee you are."

Choo Choo: The Story of a Little Engine who Ran Away

———————————————— * ————————————————

Once upon a time there was a little engine. Her name was CHOO CHOO. She was a beautiful little engine. All black and shiny. CHOO CHOO had a whistle which went "who WHOOOoo-oo-oo" when she came to the crossing. CHOO CHOO had a BELL which went DING! *DONG!* DING! *DONG!* when she came to the station. And a BRAKE which went s ss ss ss SSSSSSSSWISH!!! And just made an awful noise.

CHOO CHOO had an engineer. His name was JIM. Jim loved the little engine and took good care of her. He would shine and polish her till she looked like new and oil all the parts so they would run smoothly.

CHOO CHOO had a fireman. His name was Oley. Oley fed the little engine with coal and water. The tender carried the coal and water.

ARCHIBALD was the conductor who rode in the coaches. He took the tickets from the passengers. Archibald had a big watch. He told the little engine when it was time to start.

CHOO CHOO pulled all the coaches full of people, the luggage van full of mail and baggage, and the tender, from the little station in the little town to the big station in the big city and back again. CHOO CHOO went through the fields and across the highway where the gates were down. CHOO CHOO stopped at the little stations on the way to pick up passengers and baggage and mail to take to the big city. Ding dong! Ding dong! And she's off again. Through the tunnel and over the hills. Down the hills, across the drawbridge, and into the big station in the big city.

One day CHOO CHOO said to herself, "I am tired of pulling all these heavy coaches. I could go much faster and easier by myself, then all the people would stop and look at me, just me, and they would say, "What a smart little engine! What a fast little engine! What a beautiful little engine! Just watch her go by herself!"

The next day CHOO CHOO was left alone on the tracks while Jim and Oley and Archibald were having a cup of coffee in the restaurant. "Now is my chance!" said CHOO CHOO, and off she started. CHOO choo choochoo choo choo! CHOO choo choo choo choo choo! CHOO choo choo choo! CHOO choo choo choo! DING dong! DING dong! Who WHOOOOOOOO! STOP everyone! LOOK everyone! Stop, look and listen to ME! CHOO CHOO raced through the fields and she frightened all the cows and the horses and the chickens.

CHOO CHOO frightened all the people and some clambered up the steeple. Choo choo CHOO choo! Choo choo CHOO choo! Choo choo CHOO choo! Choo choo CHOO choo! CHOO choo CHOO!

CHOO CHOO whizzed by the crossings. All the automobiles and trucks had to put on their brakes so quickly that they piled one on top of another. My! they were mad at CHOO CHOO.

Over the hills went the little engine. Faster and faster. She couldn't stop now if she wanted to. The drawbridge was up! CHOO CHOO jumped and just made it. But she lost the tender. Fortunately it fell on a coal barge which was passing

under the drawbridge.

CHOO CHOO raced on into the big yard in the big city. Swish! Swish! went the air brakes on the express trains. Poor CHOO CHOO didn't know which way to turn. Ah! There was a track out, a freight track that ran around the city. CHOO CHOO took it and escaped.

On and on went CHOO CHOO, out of the city, through the suburbs and into the country. It was getting dark! . . . She had lost her way! . . . She did not have much coal or water left as she had lost her tender. . . . Finally she came to where the tracks divided. One track went one way and the other track the other way. She did not know which track to take so she took the track that went the other way.

It was an old old track that hadn't been used for years. Bushes and weeds had grown between the lines. The trees had spread their branches over it. It was up hill and almost dark now . . . and this is how the poor tired little engine went.

CHOOO choo choo choo ch ch CHOOoo. . . . choo. . . . .

choo choooo .... choo ... ch ... ch ch ... ch .... ch ....ch. a a a a a AH CHOO! And there she sat!

In the meantime when Jim and Oley and Archibald heard the little engine go by they jumped up and ran after her. Jim called STOP! STOP! But CHOO CHOO was too far away to hear even if she wanted to.

Jim and Oley and Archibald ran and ran till they could run no more. Just then a Streamliner train came round the corner behind them. Jim took his red handkerchief and flagged it.

The Streamliner stopped, Jim called to the Streamliner engineer, "Help me catch my runaway engine." "What about my schedule?" said the Streamliner engineer. "Never mind your schedule," said Jim. "I must find CHOO CHOO." So he climbed in and Oley and Archibald followed. Jim took the controls and ZOOM! They were off!

It was easy to see which way CHOO CHOO had gone. All the cows, horses and chickens pointed with their tails or heads. The people at the crossing cried out, "She went that way, that way! Bring her back!" And the people in the town said, "Hurry! Hurry! Hurry and catch the little engine, the naughty, runaway engine before she does any more harm."

While waiting for the drawbridge to close, Oley cried out, "Look! There's the tender in that coal barge." Jim said, "Oley and Archibald, you stay here and get the tender up. I'll go on till I find CHOO CHOO."

Archibald telephoned for the train derrick. After it came it didn't take long to get the tender back on the tracks. They all went on to the "yard" by the big station to wait for Jim to come back with CHOO CHOO.

At last they came to the place where the tracks divided. They didn't know which way to go now. While they were deciding, an old man, who used to be an engineer when he was young, called out to them, "If you're looking for a runaway engine she's right up that track there. And she won't be far as it's an old track which hasn't been used for well nigh forty years."

They turned on the big head light and went slowly up the old track. They didn't go far before they saw the little engine. CHOO CHOO was so glad to be found that she blew one

"Toot" with her whistle. There was just enough steam left for one small "Toot". Jim took a big chain and ran to the little engine and hooked it on.

The Streamliner backed down the old track, pulling CHOO CHOO back to the main track, back through the big city and back into the train yard where Oley and Archibald were waiting. They attached the tender and ran CHOO CHOO into the roundhouse and looked her over to see if any damage had been done. Except for being dusty and tired she was as good as ever. Jim and Oley and Archibald were so glad to have CHOO CHOO back they danced a jig together.

On the way home CHOO CHOO said to Jim, "I am not going to run away any more. It isn't much fun. I am going to pull all the coaches full of people and the baggage car from the little town to the big city and back again."

The Sick Cow

———————————— * ————————————

One early morning Bobby Brewster was going round a farm with the farmer, when they saw a cow looking very doleful and sorry for herself.

"Good morning, cow," said the farmer.

The cow looked up sadly.

"Bow-wow-wow," she said.

"I beg your pardon?" said the farmer.

"Bow-wow-wow," said the cow.

The farmer looked at Bobby, and Bobby looked at the farmer. They didn't want to hurt the cow's feelings, so they walked quietly away to the other side of the field.

"Did you hear what I heard?" said the farmer.

"Well, I thought I heard that cow say Bow-wow-wow," said Bobby.

"It seems a very odd thing," said the farmer. "I think we'd better give her some cow medicine."

So they went over to the barn, and the farmer found a big spoon, and a bottle with some very funny-looking stuff in it. Then they went back to the cow.

Do you think they could persuade her to take that medicine? They tried every way they could think of, but it was no use. The cow wouldn't open her mouth—at least, only once, and that was to say "bow-wow". They nearly got the spoon in between the

Bow and the Wow, but they hadn't quite got time. In the end they had to give it up as a bad job.

"I think we'd better send for a cow doctor," said the farmer.
So they did.

Luckily the cow doctor didn't live very far away, and he soon arrived on his bicycle, with his little black bag.

"Good morning. Good morning. Good morning," he said. He always tried to be cheerful at his work, because sick cows look so very sorry for themselves, with their big brown eyes.

The cow looked up.

"Well," said the cow doctor. "And how are you this morning?"

"Bow-wow-wow," said the cow.

"I beg your pardon?" said the cow doctor.

"Bow-wow-wow," said the cow.

"Indeed," said the cow doctor. "I think you'd better have a pill." He turned aside to the farmer.

"It's a clear case of dogs' disease," he said.

Have you ever seen a cow take a pill? You know how difficult it is for little boys and girls, because their tongues get in the way. Well, think how much larger a cow's tongue is than a little boy's or girl's.

This cow doctor was very clever though. He got a glass tube, and put the pill—quite a big white one—inside the tube. Then he asked the farmer to open the cow's mouth with his hands, put one end of the tube inside her mouth, and did a big blow down the other. Whoof. The pill went shooting down the cow's throat and right into her tummy before she could even cough.

As soon as it was over she closed her eyes and went off to sleep.

"Ssh," said the farmer, and they tiptoed away to the other side of the field.

"I'll call again in the morning," said the cow doctor. "In the meantime please keep her quiet and comfortable."

So they did.

The Sick Cow

The next morning the cow doctor came again as he had promised.

The cow still looked very sad.

"Well," said the cow doctor. "And are we any better this morning?"

The cow looked up.

"Miaow," she said.

"I beg your pardon?" said the cow doctor.

"Miaow," said the cow.

"This seems very complicated," said the cow doctor to the farmer. "I can't understand it at all. Yesterday it was a clear case of dogs' disease so I gave her a dogs' disease pill. Now she seems to have cats' disease. I think I'd better give her a cats' disease pill just to keep her quiet, and then we'll send for a cow specialist."

So they did.

The cow specialist had to come all the way from Vienna, so he came by helicopter and didn't arrive till the afternoon. He wore horn-rimmed spectacles and looked very clever. As soon as he landed—in a field not very far away—he hurried over to see the cow.

"How now, cow?" said the cow specialist.

I don't expect you can guess what the cow answered, can you? In fact I'm sure you can't.

She said "Quack-quack-quack."

The cow specialist didn't look in the least bit surprised, which rather disappointed the cow, because she had hoped to cause quite a stir with her quack quacking.

"Get up," said the cow specialist.

He had such a stern way with him that the cow thought she'd better do as she was told.

"Now run round the field," said the cow specialist.

The Sick Cow

Running round a field was the last thing the cow felt like doing—but she ran. When she had reached a cluster of thistles the specialist suddenly shouted "Sit down"—and down she sat, plomp in the middle of the thistles.

"Mooooh," she said, and jumped ten feet in the air.

"I beg your pardon?" said the cow specialist.

"Mooooh," said the cow.

"Repeat that, please," said the cow specialist.

"Mooooh," said the cow—much more loudly, and from that day to this she has never said anything else but "Mooooh"— which all goes to prove what a clever cow specialist that cow specialist is, now doesn't it?

Of course the farmer was delighted, and so he invited the cow specialist, the cow doctor, AND Bobby Brewster home to the farm for tea.

Can you guess what they had to eat?

Sardines!

Teddy Robinson and the Band

———————————— ✳ ————————————

One day Teddy Robinson and Deborah and Mummy all went off to spend the afternoon in the park.

When they got there Mummy found a comfortable seat to sit on and settled down to knit. Deborah and Teddy Robinson sat down on the other end of the seat and looked around to see what they could see.

Not far away some children were skipping on the grass. After she had watched them for a little while Deborah said, "I think I'd like to go and skip with those children, Teddy Robinson. You wouldn't mind staying here with Mummy, would you?"

And Teddy Robinson said, "No, I don't mind. I don't care about skipping myself, but you go. I'll watch you."

So Deborah ran off to join the other children on the grass, and Teddy Robinson and Mummy stayed sitting on the seat in the sunshine.

Soon a lady came along, holding a very little boy by the hand. As soon as she saw Mummy the lady said, "Oh, how nice to meet you here!" And she sat down beside her and started talking, because she was a friend of hers.

The very little boy, whose name was James, stared hard and said nothing.

"Look, James, this is Teddy Robinson," said Mummy. "Perhaps you would like to sit up beside him and talk to him."

Teddy Robinson and the Band

So James climbed up on the seat, and he and Teddy Robinson sat side by side and looked at each other, but neither of them said a word. They were both rather shy.

Mummy and the lady talked and talked and were very jolly together, but James and Teddy Robinson sat and did nothing and were rather dull together.

After a while James grew tired of sitting still, so he climbed down off the seat, and when nobody was looking he lifted Teddy Robinson down too, and toddled away with him.

"I hope you aren't going to lose us," said Teddy Robinson. But James said nothing at all.

They hadn't gone far before they came to some trees, and on the other side of the trees they saw a bandstand with rows of chairs all round it. It was like a little round summer-house, with open sides and a roof on top.

James and Teddy Robinson went over to look at it, and, as there was nobody there, they were able to go right up the steps and look inside. After that they ran in and out along the rows of

66

empty chairs, until they came to the back row, just under the trees. Then James sat Teddy Robinson down on one of the chairs, and sat himself down on the one next to him.

"I'm glad I've got a chair to myself," said Teddy Robinson. "It would be a pity to share one when there are so many."

But James didn't like sitting still for long. A moment later he got up again, and, forgetting all about Teddy Robinson, he ran back to the seat where Mummy and the lady were still talking. He was only a very little boy.

Teddy Robinson didn't mind at all. He felt rather grand sitting there all by himself on a chair of his own, with rows and rows of empty chairs standing all round him, and he began to think how nice it would be if someone should happen to pass by and notice him.

He looked up into the leafy branches over his head, so that people would think he was just sitting there thinking, and wouldn't guess that he had really been left there by mistake. And then he began thinking of all the things that people might say to each other when they saw him.

"Look over there!
Look where?
Why, there.
Take care, don't stare,
but alone on that chair
there's a teddy bear!
I do declare!
A bear on a chair
with his head in the air!
How *did* he get there?"

He said this to himself several times over, and then he went on:

"You can see that he's thinking
(not preening or prinking,
or winking or blinking,
or prowling or slinking,
or eating or drinking),
but just sitting thinking. . . ."

But he didn't think this was very good, and anyway he was getting into rather a muddle with so much thinking about thinking. So he was quite pleased when suddenly there was a rustling in the leaves over his head, and a sparrow hopped along the branch nearest to him and stared down at him with bright, beady eyes.

"Good afternoon," chirped the sparrow. "Are you waiting for the music?"

"Good afternoon," said Teddy Robinson. "What music?"

"The band," said the sparrow. "I thought perhaps you had

come to sing with the band. It always plays here in the afternoons."

"Oh," said Teddy Robinson, "how very nice that will be! I love singing."

"So do I," chirped the sparrow. "We all do. There are quite a lot of us up in this tree, and we sing with the band every afternoon. I really don't know how they would manage without us. I'm sure people would miss us if we didn't join in."

"How very jolly!" said Teddy Robinson. "When will the music begin?"

"Oh, very soon now," said the sparrow. "You'll see the chairs will soon begin to fill up, and then the band will arrive. Have you paid for your chair?"

"Oh, no," said Teddy Robinson. "Do I have to pay? I don't really want to buy it, only to sit in it for a little while."

"Yes, but you have to pay just to sit in it," said the sparrow. "The ticket-man will be along in a minute. You'd better pretend to be asleep."

But Teddy Robinson was far too excited to pretend to be asleep. He was longing for the band to come and for the music to begin.

Before long one or two people came along and sat down in chairs near by; then two or three more people came, and after that more and more, until nearly all the rows of chairs were full. Several people looked as if they were just going to sit down in Teddy Robinson's chair, but they saw him just in time and moved on.

Then along came the ticket-man. Teddy Robinson began to feel rather worried when he saw all the people giving him money for their seats. But it was quite all right; the man came up to where he was sitting and stopped for a moment, then he smiled at Teddy Robinson and said, "I suppose it's no use asking *you* to buy a ticket," and went away.

Teddy Robinson was very glad.

"Was it all right?" asked the sparrow, peeping through the leaves.

"Yes," said Teddy Robinson. "I don't know how he knew I hadn't any money, but it's very nice for me, because now every one will think I paid for my chair."

He sat up straighter than ever, and started to have a little think about how nice it was, to be sitting in a chair and looking as though you'd paid for it:

> "Look at that bear!
> He's paid for a chair;
> no wonder he looks so grand;
> with his paws in his lap,
> what a sensible chap!
> He's waiting to hear the band."

And then the band arrived. The men wore red and gold uniforms, and they climbed up the steps to the bandstand, carrying their trumpets and flutes and a great big drum.

"Here they come!" chirped the sparrow from the tree. "I must go and make sure the birds are all ready to start singing. Don't forget to join in yourself if you feel like it. Do you sing bass?"

"I don't know what that means," said Teddy Robinson.

"Rather deep and growly," said the sparrow.

"Oh, yes, I think perhaps I do," said Teddy Robinson.

"Good," said the sparrow. "We birds all sing soprano (that means rather high and twittery). We could do with a good bass voice." And he flew back into the tree again.

Then the band began to play.

The music went so fast that at first Teddy Robinson hadn't time to think of any words for it, so he just hummed happily to himself, and felt as if both he and the chair were jigging up and down in time to the music. Even the flies and bees began buzzing, and the birds were chirping so merrily, and the band was playing so loudly, that soon Teddy Robinson found some words to sing after all. They went like this:

"Trill-trill-trill
goes the man with the flute,
and the man with the trumpet
goes toot-toot-toot.
Cheep-cheep-cheep
go the birds in the trees,
and buzz-buzz-buzz
go the flies and the bees.
Mmmm-mmmm-mmmm
goes the teddy bear's hum,
and boom-boom-boom
goes the big bass drum."

When the music stopped every one clapped hard; but Teddy Robinson didn't clap, because, as he had been singing with the band, he was afraid it might look as if he were clapping himself.

He was just wondering whether he ought to get up and bow, as the leader of the band was doing, when he suddenly saw Deborah walking along between the rows of chairs.

She *was* surprised when she saw Teddy Robinson sitting among all the grown-up people.

"*However* did you get here?" she said. "And why didn't I know? And fancy you having a chair all to yourself!"

"What a pity you didn't come before!" said Teddy Robinson. "I've just been singing with the band. Did you hear every one clapping?"

"Yes," said Deborah, "but I'd no idea they were clapping for

you. I thought it was for the band."

"Me *and* the band," said Teddy Robinson, "and the sparrows as well. They've been singing quite beautifully."

"I *am* sorry I missed it," said Deborah. "I was skipping with the other children when somebody said the band had come, and I came over to see. I thought you were still sitting on the seat with Mummy."

"James and I got tired of it," said Teddy Robinson, "so we came over here, and then James went back, so I stayed by myself. But you haven't missed all of it. Let's stay together and hear some more."

Then Teddy Robinson moved up so that Deborah could share his chair.

"I do think you're a clever bear," she said. "I always knew you could sing very nicely, but I never thought I should find you singing with a proper band, and with every one clapping you!"

And that is the end of the story about
Teddy Robinson and the band.

The Very Young Elephant

———————————— * ————————————

O nce there was an elephant, a very young and in-experienced elephant, who lived with his gentle mother and his understanding father in the middle of the jungle. He loved his parents very dearly, and his name was Tum Tum.

One day his parents said to him, "Tum Tum, it is a very hot day, and if we should happen to doze off you must be a good son and keep out of trouble."

After a while they did doze off, and Tum Tum said to him-self: "I don't want to sleep, but it is far too hot to play games. I will walk down this shaded track under the trees and keep cool until my gentle mother and my understanding father wake up."

So he walked down the jungle track. But still he felt hot. Then he met a wart-hog. "Good day, Wart-hog," said Tum Tum. "Can you tell me the best way to keep cool on such a hot day as this?"

"Grunt!" said the wart-hog. "Grunt grunt oink grumble. Dig in the ground. Dig in the earth and bury yourself half under a log. In the cool dirt you'll feel better."

"My feet don't dig very well, and I wouldn't fit under a log," said Tum Tum. "But thank you for the advice."

"It's not much use if you can't take it," said the wart-hog. "Oink! Grumble. Guff guff."

The Very Young Elephant

And the young elephant went on his way.

The next person he met was Monkey. "Good day, Monkey," he said. "Can you tell me the way to keep cool on such a hot day as this?"

"Swing through the branches. Swing by your tail. Jump from tree to tree. The wind will whistle past your ears as you go. You have very big ears—you'll soon feel cool."

"My tail isn't strong enough to hold me up," said Tum Tum. "If I sat in a tree I'd break the branches."

"Oh well, I can only tell you what I do," said the monkey. "It's not my fault if you can't follow my advice." And he went off chattering shrilly to himself.

And it was still a very hot day.

Tum Tum was just about to turn a corner when he saw two cold, bright eyes watching him in the grass. Around the eyes was a tawny face with black spots. Tum Tum knew who that was. "Good day, Leopard," he said. "How are you this very hot day? Can you tell me how to keep cool?"

Leopard pressed back his ears against his head and opened his toothy mouth just wide enough for the words to come out. "Come into the cool grass, little elephant. Lie in the grass with me in the shade of this rock. Then you won't feel the heat any more." And Leopard licked his lips.

"No, thank you," answered Tum Tum. "I may be young and I am hot, but I'm not as silly as that. Be very careful, Leopard, or my understanding father might put his foot on you." And he trotted very quickly out of harm's way.

Presently he heard the noise of large wings flapping overhead. He looked up. There in a tree was Eagle.

"Good day, Eagle bird," he said. "Can you tell me how to keep cool in this hot weather?"

Eagle looked at him very fiercely and said: "Fly. Jump in the air and fly. Sail up into the sky, up and up in circles. There the

74

winds from the north and the south, the east and the west, will
blow on you. There you will be cool."

"I wish I could," said Tum Tum. "But I haven't any wings,
and I can't jump high enough without them."

75

The Very Young Elephant

By this time, the little elephant was beginning to feel that he might never be cool again, and then he met the Heron bird. He said to the Heron bird: "I have asked the wart-hog how to keep cool, and I have asked Monkey and Leopard and Eagle how to be cool, and none of them can tell me how to do it. They can only tell me what they do themselves."

"And that's all I can do, too," said Heron bird. "But I think you'll enjoy it. Come with me."

So Tum Tum padded along on his thick little legs behind

The Very Young Elephant

Heron bird. Down the jungle track they went, downhill all the way until Tum Tum heard the sound of water running, and in between the tree trunks he saw ahead of him the wide, silver-flowing, sunlight-dappled river. The jungle trees grew down to the water's edge, and here the Heron bird stopped.

"Now," he said, "this is how I keep cool. And this is where I have my lunch, too!" He suddenly popped his long beak down into the water and brought it out again with a small, plump fish in it.

"I don't eat fish," said Tum Tum.

"Of course not," said Heron bird. "But you do want to keep cool, don't you? Step into the water and you'll find out how to do it."

Tum Tum put one thick little leg into the river, and then another. And then he walked right into the water with all four legs. The water was cool, so cool, and the mud made squuggly noises in between his toes. "This is good!" he told Heron bird.

"Of course it is, young elephant," said Heron. "Now, you must suck up a trunk full of water and give yourself a shower-bath—and see how cool that is."

The little elephant did just that. He sucked up water and he showered his back until the water rolled down his shoulders and over his tail. Then he rolled in the mud and wallowed in the shallows and trumpeted and squealed just like a grown-up elephant. He had never had so much fun before—and he didn't feel hot any more.

The sun went down towards the mountains. Feeling cool and

comfortable, Tum Tum thanked Heron bird and went home along the jungle track to his gentle mother and his understanding father. They were surprised and pleased when they heard that their baby elephant had found out how to keep cool on a very hot day, and they all had fresh young tender leaves and green jungle grass for tea.

The Little Small Wee Tiny Man

---------------------------- * ----------------------------

Once upon a time there was a little, small, wee, tiny man. So small, so very, very small. Why, he was only SO big!

And he lived all alone in a little house, such a little, small, wee, tiny house it was. Why, his house was only THAT big.

And every day he went out and picked one grain of wheat and ground it up to make his loaf of bread. And he filled his little bucket with one drop of dew, and one stewed blackberry gave him puddings for a week. And he had a good appetite for such a very little, small, wee, tiny man.

But he lived all alone and that made him very sad. And he cried and cried and One, Two, Three, Four, Five! Five little, small, wee, tiny tears fell from his eyes and rolled down his cheeks and splashed one, two, three, four, five, five little splashes on the floor.

So then it got known that the little, small, wee, tiny man was sad at living alone and was sitting indoors all day crying and crying.

So one day a child came to the place where the little, small, wee, tiny house was standing, and after looking round and about very hard the child saw it and knelt down.

Now the child was SO big; and therefore spoke very, very softly so as not to frighten the little, small, wee, tiny man.

"Little man, little man, shall I come and live with you?"

But though the child spoke so softly, to the little, small, wee, tiny man it sounded like this.

"LITTLE MAN, LITTLE MAN, SHALL I COME AND LIVE WITH YOU?"

And the little, small, wee, tiny man was so frightened he ran and shut the door and shut all the windows and ran and crept under his little, small, wee, tiny bed, and putting his hands to his mouth cried out as loud as he could:

"Go away, go away. You are MUCH too big!"

But so loud as he shouted all the child heard was a little, small, wee, tiny squeaking like the voice of a mosquito— eeeeeeeeeeeeeee.

So the child got up and went away.

And the little, small, wee, tiny man came out from under the bed and began to cry. One, two, three, four, five little tears made one, two, three, four, five little splashes on the floor.

Next came a cat who at once saw the little small, wee, tiny house because being a cat, her eyes were very sharp. She was a black cat and so big.

And she said very softly, so as not to frighten the little, small, wee, tiny man:

"Miaow, miaow. Little man, little man. Shall I come and live with you?"

But though the cat spoke so softly, to the little, small, wee, tiny man it sounded like this:

"MIAOW, MIAOW. LITTLE MAN, LITTLE MAN, SHALL I COME AND LIVE WITH YOU?"

And the little, small, wee, tiny man was so frightened he ran to the window to see what this might be, and all he saw was a HUGE yellow eye, and it quite filled the whole window pane. So then he was so frightened he pulled the curtains over the window and crept under his little, small, wee, tiny bed and put

his hands to his mouth and shouted at the top of his voice:

"Go away, go away. You are MUCH too big."

But so loud as he shouted all the cat could hear was a little, small, wee squeaking like the voice of a mosquito—eeeeeeeeeeee.

So the cat got up and went away.

And the little, small, wee tiny man came out from under the bed and began to cry. One, two, three, four, five little tears made one, two, three, four, five little splashes on the floor.

Next there came a mouse, and not a very big mouse either, for she was only so big. And she did not take long to find the little house for she smelt his bread baking in the oven. And up she went, sniff sniff sniffing to the door, and spoke very softly so as not to frighten the little, small, wee, tiny man.

"Squeak, squeak. Little man, little man, shall I come and live with you?"

But so softly though she spoke, to the little, small, wee, tiny man it sounded like this.

"SQUEAK SQUEAK. LITTLE MAN, LITTLE MAN, SHALL I COME AND LIVE WITH YOU?"

And the little, small, wee, tiny man was so frightened he ran to the window to see what it might be, and he saw a huge, wet, grey, whiskery nose and it quite filled the whole window. So then he was so frightened he shut the shutters and ran as quick as he could and crept under the bed and putting his hands to his mouth he shouted as loud as he could:

"Go away, go away, you are MUCH too big."

But so loud as he shouted all the mouse could hear was a little, small, wee, tiny squeaking like the voice of a mosquito—eeeeeeeeeeee.

So the mouse got up and went away.

The Little Small Wee Tiny Man

And the little, wee, small, tiny man came out from under the bed and began to cry. One, two, three, four, five little tears made one, two, three, four, five little splashes on the floor.

But now there came an ant, and when she saw the little, small, wee, tiny house she said to herself:

"Oh my, oh my, what a very fine gentleman he must be to live in such a fine big house."

And she went to the door and rang the little bell rather timidly, ting ting ting.

The little, small, wee, tiny man went to the door and opened it. There he saw the ant and such a nice little, small, wee, tiny creature she looked with her shiny red skin and her pretty little legs and her tiny waving antennae; he liked her at once.

And when she said in a clear voice:

"Good sir, I hope you will not think me too bold if I suggest coming to live with you," and it sounded to him just like this:

"Good sir, I hope you will not think me too bold if I suggest coming to live with you," he answered at once:

"Oh, you lovely little creature, come in, come in. I have been so sad all alone in my little, small, wee, tiny house. But if you will come and live with me, why, then we can both be happy from morning till night."

And the ant went in and ran all over the house and thought it the very grandest place she had ever been in.

So ever after that the little, small, wee, tiny man picked Two grains of wheat every day and made Two little loaves for himself and the ant. And he went out twice and filled his little bucket with Two drops of dew, and as for pudding he had to pick three big blackberries instead of only one for the ant was very fond of her pudding and ate it all up every day!

So the little, small, wee, tiny man never again shed one, two, three, four, five little tears but lived happily ever after with the even smaller, wee-er, tinier, extremely little Ant!

Teddy Bear Meets Zoo Bear

---------------------------------- * ----------------------------------

One day when Mummy was hanging out the washing, Sally had the bright idea of giving Teddy a bath. He had become very grubby, not having had a bath since Uncle John had sent him to her on her fifth birthday, and the other dolls didn't like playing with him.

"Can I have a bowl of warm water, Mummy?" she asked. "I want to give Teddy a wash."

"Yes," Mummy answered, "and you'd better have soap and a flannel too."

With this, Sally washed Teddy very carefully all over. Then taking a length of red ribbon, one of her own that she used for her hair, she tied it securely round Teddy's waist and hung him up on the line outside.

It was a very cold day and the wind blew hard, but the sun shone brightly all around.

Mummy had said: "It's a good day for drying", so Sally went indoors and watched Teddy swinging in the wind at the end of her ribbon.

She noticed he was dripping quite a lot from his hands and legs, and from his eyes and ears too, because Sally hadn't been able to squeeze him very hard, and of course she could not put him through the mangle!

She felt rather sorry for him, swaying so helplessly in the cold wind. "But he'll soon dry," she thought to herself, "and be glad to be welcomed back into the toy cupboard all nice and clean with all the other dolls."

Sally sat on the broad window sill and watched Teddy getting dry. After a little while she grew tired of this and dropped off to sleep. Just then, who should come walking down the garden towards the washing line but a sweet baby bear—a real one this time!

When he got to where Teddy was hanging, he stopped and looked up at him with large tender eyes. Teddy stopped swinging and gave a squeak of delight.

"Good morning," said the real bear timidly.

"Hello," answered Teddy. "I'm sorry I'm not on my feet to welcome you, but you see my mistress Sally decided to give me a bath today."

"Oh don't worry about that," said the bear. "I'm Raymond. Shall I help you to get down? I've something important to tell you."

"Well, no," replied Teddy, not quite knowing what to say. "I think Sally might be cross if I get down before I'm dry."

Raymond looked as if he were going to cry, so Teddy said: "Well, if it really is important, perhaps I'd better come down after all. Just untie this red ribbon, please."

Raymond reached up and quickly undid the knot.

"That's better," said Teddy. "It wasn't very pleasant hanging up there. But I never complain. It's nicer to be clean than to be dirty."

Then he stopped so that Raymond could tell him about the important news. But the real bear was looking at him, rather puzzled.

"Excuse me saying so," he began, "but isn't it a strain to stand on your hind legs like that all the time?"

"No, not at all," answered Teddy. "I'm quite used to it now.

I use my front legs as arms and hands, just as my mistress does."

"Oh, I see," said Raymond. "But anyway, do please listen to me. You are still a bear, aren't you, no matter how you may choose to stand? And we bears must stick together in times of trouble. I'm in a spot of bother."

"Tell me what is wrong," said Teddy. "Perhaps I can help you. Sally always confides in me when she's worried about something."

"Well, it's like this," said Raymond. "I've just run away from the zoo."

"Oooh!" gasped Teddy, "Have you really? That's *very* serious."

"Yes, I know it's rather naughty of me," answered the real little bear. "But there it is. Jimmy, my keeper, left the cage door open one afternoon, and I just slipped out. I didn't mean to go far, but there were so many things to see, and I lost my way. It was then I saw you through the trees at the end of your garden, and I thought I'd come and ask your advice about getting back. I'm really very happy at the zoo. All my friends are there."

"All right. Now you just wait here, Raymond," said Teddy, "and I'll go and fetch Sally. She'll soon tell you what to do. She's a very clever girl."

"Oh no!" cried the baby bear. He was frightened of human beings. "I'd rather not bring her into it. Besides, she might have me punished."

Teddy simply smiled at Raymond's fears. "You wait here," he said. "Don't be afraid. I'll be back in a jiffy."

Raymond sat down, his heart beating fast. In a few moments out came Teddy. He was pulling Sally by the hand. She gave a whoop of delight when she caught sight of the soft brown baby bear. She came and stroked his back while Teddy told her the whole story. Raymond didn't seem frightened now.

"Well, what do you think, Sally?" asked Teddy when he had

finished. "What do you think Raymond ought to do?"

"Well," she said, "there's no doubt at all about what he must do. I'm terribly sorry to have to say so, but he must go back to the zoo at once."

"Oh dear," said Teddy, looking very sad. But he knew it was no use to argue with his mistress.

"I know—I'll go indoors and speak to Mummy," she told him, "and if she's willing, we'll all take Raymond back after tea. But I hope Jimmy your keeper isn't too worried. By the way, Teddy my dear, are you quite dry?" She felt at the smooth fur on his back. "Yes," she said, "I think you are just about ready."

So the three of them went into the house. Sally's mother was very surprised to see a live little bear, and she agreed with Sally about taking Raymond back right away.

Teddy Bear Meets Zoo Bear

"The people at the zoo will be searching everywhere, wondering what can have happened to you, especially with so many motor cars running around these days. It will be far safer for you to stay in the zoo, and not to run away, ' she said.

Sally said: "Teddy has become very fond of Raymond, Mummy. Shall we be able to go and see him at the zoo?"

"Of course we shall," she said. "But come along everybody, we'd better be off now."

The four of them went out and got on a bus. Mummy nursed Raymond all the way until they arrived at the zoo.

Jimmy the keeper came smiling to meet them. He took Raymond from Sally's mother and showed him to Mrs. Bear, who was looking at them through the bars of her cage. The keeper gave Sally a free ticket to come to the zoo whenever she liked, and one for Teddy as well.

The Lion who couldn't Roar

———————————— * ————————————

Once there was a little lion who lived in the forest with his father and mother.

When Father Lion had been out hunting, and roared to let Mother Lion know he was coming home, you could hear him all over the forest. And when Mother Lion roared back, you could hear *her* all over the forest. But the little lion had just a little voice.

"Never mind," said Mother Lion. "As you grow bigger, your voice will grow bigger, too."

But it didn't.

One day Uncle Lion came to visit.

"We are glad to see you," roared Mother Lion.

"Where have you been all this time?" roared Father Lion.

"Been on my summer holiday hunting trip," roared Uncle Lion. "And how are you, young fellow?"

"Very well, thank you," said the little lion in his little voice.

"Bless my soul!" said Uncle Lion. "What's the matter? Lost your voice?"

"Not all of my voice," said the little lion. "Just my roar."

"High time you found it!" said Uncle Lion.

The little lion sat down and thought about what Uncle Lion had said, and after a while, when the grown ups were busy talking, he went off into the forest, all by himself.

The Lion who couldn't Roar

He saw some monkeys playing in the branches of a tall tree.

"Excuse me, please," said the little lion politely, "I've lost my voice. Not all of my voice, just my roar. Do you know where I might find it?"

The monkeys laughed till they almost fell out of the tree.

"Look at the lion without a roar!" they shouted. "Listen to his little voice! Say something more, lion!" And they swung upside down from the branches, and threw twigs and leaves down on him.

"I think you're very rude," said the little lion in his little voice, and he went away, out of the trees and down to the river.

At the edge of the river he found Mr. Hippopotamus dozing in a nice warm squishy mud bath.

"Excuse me, please," said the little lion politely, "I've lost my voice. Not all of my voice, just my roar."

Mr. Hippopotamus opened one eye. "And a good thing, too," he said. "There's too much noise around here."

"Do you know where I might find it?" asked the little lion.

"Certainly not," said Mr. Hippopotamus, "and if I did, I wouldn't tell you." And he went to sleep again.

The little lion went on through the forest till he found a pretty little green snake curled up on top of a rock.

"Excuse me, please," he said politely, "I've lost my voice. Not all of my voice, just my roar. Do you know where I might find it?"

The little snake uncurled herself slowly.

"Yes-s-s," she said at last. "I think I know the very place where you might find your roar, but it's in a very dangerous-s-s part of the forest."

"I don't mind," said the little lion bravely.

"Follow me, then," said the snake. "This-s-s way."

And she slipped down from the rock and slid away among the trees so fast that the little lion had to run to keep up with her.

Soon they came to a part of the forest where the little lion had never been before. The trees were very tall and very close together, so that it was dark underneath them, and the bushes were so thick that there was no path through them.

"This-s-s is the place," said the little snake, and she slid into the bushes and disappeared.

"Come back!" said the little lion. "Don't leave me alone here!"

But the little green snake didn't come back.

"Mother!" said the little lion in his little voice, "Mother! I don't know where I am! I think I'm lost!"

But of course Mother Lion couldn't hear him.

The little lion sat down and looked round him. It was very dark and very lonely, and he was very frightened.

So he cried. And he howled. And he ROARED.

And from far away in the forest Mother Lion roared back, "I'm here, my little son! I'm coming!"

The little green snake slid out from under the bushes where she had been hiding all the time.

"I'm s-s-sorry I s-s-scared you," she said, "but I thought you'd find your roar if you ever *really* needed it." And she disappeared again.

Then the three big lions came bounding through the forest to where the little lion was. Father Lion hugged him, and Mother Lion kissed him, and Uncle Lion said, "Bless my soul, with a roar like that you should grow up to be the biggest lion in the forest."

And they all went home together.

My Naughty Little Sister at the Party

———————————— * ————————————

You wouldn't think there could be another child as naughty as my naughty little sister, would you? But there was. There was a thoroughly bad boy who was my naughty little sister's best boyfriend, and this boy's name was Harry.

This Bad Harry and my naughty little sister used to play together quite a lot in Harry's garden, or in our garden, and got up to dreadful mischief between them, picking all the baby gooseberries, and the green black-currants, and throwing sand on the flower-beds, and digging up the runner-bean seeds, and all the naughty sorts of things you never never do in the garden.

Now, one day this Bad Harry's birthday was near, and Bad Harry's mother said he could have a birthday-party and invite lots of children to tea. So Bad Harry came round to our house with a pretty card in an envelope for my naughty little sister, and this card was an invitation asking my naughty little sister to come to the birthday-party.

Bad Harry told my naughty little sister that there would be a lovely tea with jellies and sandwiches and birthday-cake, and my naughty little sister said, "Jolly good."

And every time she thought about the party she said, "Nice tea and birthday-cake." Wasn't she greedy? And when the party day came she didn't make any fuss when my mother

95

dressed her in her new green party-dress, and her green party-shoes and her green hair-ribbon, and she didn't fidget and she didn't wriggle her head about when she was having her hair combed, she kept as still as still, because she was so pleased to think about the party, and when my mother said, "Now, what must you say at the party?" My naughty little sister said, "I must say, 'nice tea'."

But my mother said, "No, no, that *would* be a greedy thing to say. You must say 'please' and 'thank you' like a good polite child, at tea-time, and say 'thank you very much for having me', when the party is over."

And my naughty little sister said, "All right, Mother, I promise."

So, my mother took my naughty little sister to the party, and what do you think the silly little girl did as soon as she got there? She went up to Bad Harry's mother and she said very quickly, "Please-and-thank-you, and-thank-you-very-much for-having-me" all at once—just like that, before she forgot to be polite, and then she said, "Now, may I have a lovely tea?"

Wasn't that rude and greedy? Bad Harry's mother said, "I'm afraid you will have to wait until all the other children are here, but Harry shall show you the tea-table if you like."

Bad Harry looked very smart in a blue party-suit, with white socks and shoes and a *real man's haircut*, and he said, "Come on, I'll show you."

So they went into the tea-room and there was the birthday-tea spread out on the table. Bad Harry's mother had made red jellies and yellow jellies, and blancmanges and biscuits and sandwiches and cakes-with-cherries-on, and a big birthday-cake with white icing on it and candles and "Happy Birthday Harry", written on it.

My naughty little sister's eyes grew bigger and bigger, and Bad Harry said, "There's something else in the larder. It's going

to be a surprise treat, but you shall see it because you are my best girl-friend."

So Bad Harry took my naughty little sister out into the kitchen and they took chairs and climbed up to the larder shelf—which is a dangerous thing to do, and it would have been their own faults if they had fallen down—and Bad Harry showed my naughty little sister a lovely spongy trifle, covered with creamy stuff and with silverballs and jelly-sweets on the top. And my naughty little sister stared more than ever because she liked spongy trifle better than jellies or blancmanges or biscuits or sandwiches or cakes-with-cherries-on, or even birth-day-cake, so she said, "For me."

Bad Harry said, "For me too," because he liked spongy trifle best as well.

Then Bad Harry's mother called to them and said, "Come along, the other children are arriving."

So they went to say, "How do you do!" to the other children, and then Bad Harry's mother said, "I think we will have a few games now before tea—just until everyone has arrived."

All the other children stood in a ring and Bad Harry's mother said, "Ring O'Roses first, I think." And all the nice party children said, "Oh, we'd like that."

But my naughty little sister said, "No Ring O'Roses—nasty Ring O'Roses"—just like that, because she didn't like Ring O'Roses very much, and Bad Harry said, "Silly game." So Bad Harry and my naughty little sister stood and watched the others. The other children sang beautifully too, they sang:

"Ring O'Ring O'Roses,
A pocket full of posies—
A-tishoo, a-tishoo, we all fall down."

And they all fell down and laughed, but Harry and my naughty little sister didn't laugh. They got tired of watching and they went for a little walk. Do you know where they went to?

Yes. To the larder. To take another look at the spongy trifle. They climbed up on to the chairs to look at it really properly. It was very pretty.

"Ring O'Ring O'Roses," sang the good party children.

"Nice jelly-sweets," said my naughty little sister. "Nice silver balls," and she looked at that terribly Bad Harry and he looked at her.

"Take one," said that naughty boy, and my naughty little

sister did take one, she took a red jelly-sweet from the top of the trifle; and then Bad Harry took a green jelly-sweet; and then my naughty little sister took a yellow jelly-sweet and a silver ball, and then Bad Harry took three jelly-sweets, red, green and yellow, and six silver balls. One, two, three, four, five, six, and put them all in his mouth at once.

Now some of the creamy stuff had come off upon Bad Harry's fingers and he liked it very much, so he put his finger into the creamy stuff on the trifle, and took some of it off and ate it, and my naughty little sister ate some too. I'm sorry to have to tell you this, because I feel so ashamed of them, and expect you feel ashamed of them too.

I hope you aren't too shocked to hear any more? Because, do you know, those two bad children forgot all about the party and the nice children all singing "Ring O'Roses". They took a spoon

99

each and scraped off the creamy stuff and ate it, and then they began to eat the nice spongy inside.

Bad Harry said, "Now we've made the trifle look so untidy, no one else will want any, so we may as well eat it all up." So they dug away into the spongy inside of the trifle and found lots of nice fruity bits inside. It was a very big trifle, but those greedy children ate and ate.

Then, just as they had nearly finished the whole big trifle, the "Ring O'Roses"-ing stopped, and Bad Harry's mother called, "Where are you two? We are ready for tea."

Then my naughty little sister was very frightened. Because she knew she had been very naughty, and she looked at Bad Harry and *he* knew *he* had been very naughty, and they both felt terrible. Bad Harry had a creamy mess of trifle all over his face, and even in his real man's haircut, and my naughty little sister had made her new green party-dress all trifly—you know how it happens if you eat too quickly and greedily.

"It's tea-time," said Bad Harry, and he looked at my naughty little sister, and my naughty little sister thought of the jellies and the cakes and the sandwiches, and all the other things, and she felt very full of trifle, and she said, "Don't want any."

And do you know what she did? Just as Bad Harry's mother came into the kitchen, my naughty little sister slipped out of the door, and ran and ran all the way home. It was a good thing our home was only down the street and no roads to cross, or I don't know what would have happened to her.

Bad Harry's mother was so cross when she saw the trifle that she sent Bad Harry straight to bed, and he had to stay there and hear all the nice children enjoying themselves. I don't know what happened to him in the night, but I know that my naughty little sister wasn't at all a well girl, from having eaten so much trifle—and I also know that she doesn't like spongy trifle any more.

Little Bear Goes to the Moon

———————————— * ————————————

I have a new space helmet. I am going to the moon," said Little Bear to Mother Bear.

"How?" asked Mother Bear.

"I'm going to fly to the moon," said Little Bear.

"Fly!" said Mother Bear. "You can't fly."

"Birds fly," said Little Bear.

"Oh, yes," said Mother Bear. "Birds fly, but they don't fly to the moon. And you are not a bird."

"Maybe some birds fly to the moon, I don't know. And maybe I can fly like a bird," said Little Bear.

"And maybe," said Mother Bear, "you are a little fat bear cub with no wings and no feathers. Maybe if you jump up you will come down very fast, with a big plop."

"Maybe," said Little Bear. "But I'm going now. Just look for me up in the sky."

"Be back for lunch," said Mother Bear.

Little Bear thought: "I will jump from a good high spot, far up into the sky, and fly up, up, up. I will be going too fast to look at things, so I will shut my eyes."

Little Bear climbed to the top of a little hill, and climbed to the top of a little tree, a very little tree on the little hill, and shut his eyes and jumped.

Down, down he came with a big plop, and down the hill he

tumbled. Then he sat up and looked around.

"My, my," he said. "Here I am on the moon. The moon looks just like the earth.

"Well, well," said Little Bear. "The trees here look just like our trees. The birds look just like our birds. And look at this," he said.

"Here is a house that looks just like my house. I'll go in and see what kind of bears live here."

"Look at that," said Little Bear. "Something to eat is on the table. It looks like a good lunch for a little bear."

Mother Bear came in and said, "But who is this? Are you a bear from earth?"

"Oh, yes, I am," said Little Bear. "I climbed a little hill, and jumped from a little tree, and flew here, just like the birds."

"Well," said Mother Bear, "my little bear did the same thing. He put on his space helmet and flew to earth. So I guess you can have his lunch."

Little Bear put his arms round Mother Bear. He said, "Mother Bear, stop fooling. You are my Mother Bear and I am your Little Bear, and we are on earth, and you know it. Now may I eat my lunch?"

"Yes," said Mother Bear, "and then you will have your nap. For you are my little bear, and I know it."

The Cat Sat on the Mat

———————————*———————————

The cat sat on the mat. Lots of cats do that, everybody knows. And nothing strange comes of it. But once a cat sat on a mat and something strange did come of it.

This is how it all began.

There was once a little girl called Emma Pippin. She had red rosy cheeks and brown hair and she lived with her Aunt Lou. They were very poor, too poor to buy a house, so they lived in an old bus. The engine would not go, but it was a nice old bus and they loved it. The outside of the bus was painted blue, the inside was painted white, and the windows had orange curtains. There was a stove, which kept them warm, and the smoke went out of a chimney in the roof.

Look at the picture and you'll see what the bus was like.

It stood by a high white wall. Inside this wall were many lovely green apple trees, on which were growing many lovely red apples. The apple trees were owned by a proud, grand man called Sir Laxton Superb.

Every day Aunt Lou went through a door into the orchard to work for Sir Laxton Superb. Aunt Lou picked the apples, which were sent away to shops. There were so many trees that when Aunt Lou had finished picking the last tree, the first one had apples growing on it again!

But Aunt Lou could not take any lovely red apples for herself.

The Cat Sat on the Mat

Not a single one! Sir Laxton Superb was a very mean man. He only let her take the apples that were going bad. And he only paid her a penny a day.

As for Emma, she might not even go into the orchard. She longed to go in, for Aunt Lou had told her about the green trees and the red apples, but Sir Laxton Superb said children would eat his apples, or spoil them. So Emma had to stay outside, looking at the high white wall.

She had no toys to play with. She and Aunt Lou were too poor. So she worked hard all day keeping the bus nice and clean. And she cooked dinner, ready for when Aunt Lou came home.

What did she cook? Bad Apples! She made bad-apple sauce, bad-apple cake, bad-apple pie, even bad-toffee-apples.

Emma was growing very fast. Every day she grew taller. She grew so fast that she was growing too big for her dress. And Aunt Lou was too poor to buy her a new dress. Emma's dress was so small that she could hardly move!

"If we take your dress off to wash it," Aunt Lou said, "we may not be able to get it back on again. I shall wash you and your dress both together."

So she put Emma in the bath, and she washed Emma and the dress, and hung them both on the clothes-line to dry.

Then Aunt Lou went off for the day to pick apples. "You may get down when you and your dress are dry," she said.

As Emma was swinging in the wind, a poor old fairy came along. She walked slowly with a stick, because she was so old.

When she saw Emma, swinging on the clothes-line, she started to laugh. She laughed and she laughed! She laughed so much she nearly fell over!

"Oh!" she said, when she could stop laughing. "I have never seen anyone on a clothes-line before. You can't think how funny you look!"

Emma said, "My dress is too small, so Aunt Lou washes it on me, in case I can't put it on again when I have taken it off. I'm almost dry now, so I can come down if you will help me."

The fairy helped Emma down.

"Would you like to come into our bus," Emma said, "and have some bad-apple cake?"

"Thank you," said the fairy. "I should like to very much. I have never been in a bus." The fairy thought the bus was lovely. And she had three helpings of bad-apple cake. She said it was very good! She told Emma,

"You have cheered me up, so I shall try to help you. I am too old and poor to give you a grand present, but I will give you

"PRIVATE
TRESPASSERS WILL
BE PROSECUTED
BY ORDER OF
SIR LAXTON
SUPERB

three of my dresses. They are too small for me now, but they will be just right for you."

So the fairy gave Emma three dresses, one red, one blue, and one grey.

"And as well as the dresses," she said, "I will give you a kitten to play with."

The kitten was called Sam, and he was black, with green eyes. Emma loved him at once, because he was so small and soft and bouncy.

Then the fairy said goodbye and walked slowly away with her stick.

Aunt Lou was very pleased when she came home and saw the dresses. She cut up the red one and the blue one, and made new dresses for Emma. They looked lovely. Aunt Lou left the grey dress, because it was not a pretty colour.

The Cat Sat on the Mat

Emma had the red dress for weekdays and the blue dress for Sundays.

As for Sam—he slept on Emma's bed every night!

"After all," Emma said to Aunt Lou, "he *is* a fairy cat."

"Fairy cat or no fairy cat," said Aunt Lou, "he has very muddy paws!"

Every night Sam left black BLACK footprints all over Emma's nice clean bed. On her sheets! And on her blankets! And on her pillow!

So Emma made a grey mat from the fairy's grey dress, and put it on her bed. And Sam jumped on to it. But on his way he walked over the pillow and left BLACK footmarks before sitting on the mat.

"Oh dear, Sam," said Emma. "You should clean your feet on your mat. I *wish* you would. What will Aunt Lou say when she comes home and sees those black marks?"

The Cat Sat on the Mat

When Emma said, "I *wish* you would," Sam stood up. He looked at Emma. Then wiped his feet on the mat! Emma *was* surprised.

"Why!" she said. "It must be a wishing-mat. What else can I wish? I wish those black, muddy marks were not on my pillow."

That very minute, Emma's pillow was clean as clean. The black marks had gone.

"Now," Emma said, "I wish I had a big meat pie and some ice-cream for Aunt Lou's dinner when she comes home."

Just as Emma said this, Sam got up. And as Emma said the word *ice*, Sam jumped off his mat.

When Emma looked on the kitchen table, there was a big meat pie and a lump of ice.

"I wished for ice-cream, not ice," said Emma. "I wish the ice would turn into ice-cream."

But the ice did not turn into ice-cream.

"I know," Emma said. "The mat is only a wishing-mat when Sam is sitting on it. Please, Sam, will you get back on your mat?"

But Sam wanted to go out, and he jumped out of the window.

"I will wish for more things when Sam comes back," Emma said.

But Aunt Lou came back before Sam.

Aunt Lou was cross, because Sir Laxton Superb had told her he did not want her shabby old bus standing by his nice white wall.

"You will have to move it to some other place," he said.

So Aunt Lou was worried. Where could they move their bus? Who could they get to help them? They were too poor to pay anybody. Aunt Lou was tired and sad, so she did not listen to what Emma was telling her.

"Aunt Lou, I've got a wishing-mat," Emma said.

"Yes, dear," Aunt Lou said, but she was not really listening.
"It gives wishes!" Emma said.

"Yes, dear," Aunt Lou said, but she was not really listening.
"It cleaned my bed. And it gave us this nice meat pie!"

"Yes, dear!" But Aunt Lou did not really hear what Emma
was saying. She ate some pie, but she was worrying so much
about how to move the bus that she never even tasted it. She
might just as well have been eating bad-apple sauce!

Aunt Lou did not tell Emma that they had to move the bus.

Grown-ups do not always tell their troubles to children, but
sometimes it would be better if they did.

Sam didn't come home all night. He went into the woods and
played puss-in-the-corner with the squirrels. By the time he
came home, Aunt Lou had gone off to pick apples.

Sam jumped up on to his mat. Emma had been waiting for
this.

"I wish I had a toy!" she said. "A skipping-rope! And some
balloons! And a ball! And a pair of skates! And a box of —"

Just then Sam jumped off his mat again. A big red ball had
rolled across the floor and he wanted to chase it.

All the things were there that Emma had wished for. The
skipping-rope. And the balloons. And the ball. And the skates.

Emma had been going to wish for a box of paints, but Sam
jumped off the mat before she had finished. So all she got was a
big empty box. She put the skates in it.

Emma had a very happy morning. She skipped and skipped
and skipped. Then she skated and skated and skated. Then she
played with the ball. Sam played with her. Then she played
with the balloons. Sam did too. This was not good for the
balloons.

At last Sam and Emma were both tired. Sam went to sleep on
the mat.

"I wish I had a paint-box!" said Emma.

The Cat Sat on the Mat

At once there was a big, lovely paint-box on the table in the bus. There were many colours in it—red, blue, green, yellow, orange, purple—all the colours you can think of!

"Oh, what lovely paints!" Emma said. "I shall paint a fine picture. I should like to paint the best picture in the whole world."

Emma looked for a bit of paper. But none of the bits of paper in the bus was big enough for the picture she wanted to paint.

"I know!" she said. "I'll paint a picture on the white wall."

So she started painting a picture on Sir Laxton Superb's high white wall. First she painted all the part she could reach. Then she climbed on a chair and painted all the high-up part of the wall.

What did Emma paint?

She painted a picture of the orchard inside the wall—the green, green trees and the red, red apples. But as she had never seen it, she painted the apples many other colours as well—pink and yellow and blue and gold and orange. Under the trees she painted foxes and squirrels and rabbits, eating bread and jelly. Birds were flying through the air, playing with balloons. Dogs were skating. Cats were skipping.

It was a very fine picture—the finest in the whole world.

And all the time, Sam went on sleeping on his mat. He was tired out.

Then Aunt Lou came through the door in the wall.

"Look, Aunt Lou!" Emma called. "Look at the lovely picture I've painted!"

But after Aunt Lou came Sir Laxton Superb.

"You must move your bus away at the end of this week!" Sir Laxton Superb was saying.

And all the time, Sam was sleeping on his mat.

Aunt Lou looked very worried. When Emma said, "Look at my lovely picture," she said, "Yes, dear," without looking. But

The Cat Sat on the Mat

Sir Laxton Superb looked. And his face went red—redder than the reddest apple you ever saw!

"*What* have you done to my lovely white wall?" he said. He looked so cross that Emma thought he might go off bang like a balloon.

"I've painted the best picture in the whole world on it," she said. "Aren't you pleased?"

But Sir Laxton Superb was not pleased. Not at all pleased!

"You must rub it all off again!" he said. "And you must leave *at once!* Today! This minute!"

Aunt Lou began to cry, "But where can we go?" she said.

"I don't care!" Sir Laxton Superb said. (And Sam was still sleeping on his mat.) "I wish the wind would blow you and your shabby old bus up into the sky!"

And Sam was *still* asleep on his mat!

The Cat Sat on the Mat

That very minute a great wind blew Aunt Lou, and Emma, and the bus, up into the air. Up they went, up, up, and up, till they landed on a fat white cloud. All the things in the bus fell about, but nothing broke. And, just think, Sam was still asleep on his mat. He was so tired after all those games.

"Well!" said Aunt Lou. "I thought of living in plenty of places, but I never thought of living up in the sky! What shall we find to eat up here?"

"That's easy," Emma said. And she wished for a roast chicken, and a big iced cake, and a jug of milk, and an orange jelly.

For Sam was still asleep on his mat!

After dinner they walked about on the cloud. It was soft— just like the hay in a hay barn. And they found lots of apples —because the wind had blown all the apples off Sir Laxton Superb's trees. They were rolling about, all over the sky!

From that day, the trees in Sir Laxton Superb's orchard never had any more apples. And although he tried to rub Emma's picture off the wall, he couldn't.

"If Sam's mat is a wishing-mat," Aunt Lou said, "we could wish our bus to be moved to California. Or Canada. Or Canton. Or the Canary Islands."

"Oh, no!" said Emma. "Let's go on living up here."

And so they did. If you look up some dark night you may get a sight of the old bus shining away up there. And you are almost sure to see some of the apples.

Zippy who Nearly Choked

---*---

One fine morning when Rita the hen was nosing about the farm-yard with her brood of yellow chicks, she suddenly heard an alarming noise. What had happened was this. Zippy, the chick who was always getting into mischief, had accidentally pecked at a bean and it had stuck in her throat. Poor Zippy was choking and making the most peculiar noises. Then she fell to the ground and lay there almost without breathing. Rita knew that the only thing that would get the bean safely down Zippy's throat was a pat of butter. So off she ran to the cow.

"Oh cow," she said, "do give me some butter. My poor Zippy is lying there choking, with a bean stuck in her throat."

Zippy who Nearly Choked

The cow said, "If you get me some hay from the haymakers, I'll give you some butter." So Rita ran to the haymakers.

"Please give me some hay for the cow," she said. "And she will then give me some butter for my Zippy who is lying in the farmyard choking with a bean stuck down her throat."

Said the haymakers: "If you get us some buns from the baker's we'll be glad to give you some hay."

Off went Rita to the baker.

"Would you kindly give me some buns to give to the haymakers," she pleaded. "They will then give me some hay to give to the cow, who will then give me some butter for my poor Zippy who is lying over there nearly choking to death with a bean in her throat."

The baker replied: "First get me some firewood from the woodcutter."

So Rita ran off to the woodcutter and said to him, "Please give me some firewood to give to the baker so that he can bake

some buns which I must give to the haymakers, who will then give me some hay to give to the cow, who will then give me some butter to save the life of my poor Zippy, who is lying in the farm-yard choking to death with a bean stuck in her throat."

The woodcutter said: "First go to the blacksmith and ask him for an axe, because I've lost mine."

Zippy who Nearly Choked

So off ran Rita to the black-smith and said, "Please give me an axe to give to the woodcutter so that he may chop some fire-wood that I can give to the baker, who will then light his fire and bake some buns, which I will then give to the haymakers, who will give me some hay to give to the cow, who will then give me the butter which I can give to my poor Zippy to help her swallow the bean which is stuck in her throat. For she is lying in the farm-yard nearly choking to death, poor little thing."

Said the blacksmith: "First get me some iron to make the axe." So Rita ran off to the little people who lived deep under the mountains and guarded all the iron down inside the earth.

"Oh little people," she said, "please give me some iron to give to the blacksmith, who will make an axe which I shall give to the woodcutter, who will chop some firewood for me to take to the baker, who will bake some buns for the haymakers, who will then give me some hay, which I can give to the cow, who will provide me with the butter to give to my poor Zippy to help her swallow the bean which is stuck in her throat and nearly choking her to death."

Zippy who Nearly Choked

The little people were most kind and felt very sorry for Rita and her little Zippy. They carried a whole heap of iron to the blacksmith. The blacksmith then made an axe for the wood-cutter. The woodcutter chopped up some firewood and took it to the baker. The baker then lit a fire with the firewood and baked his buns, which Rita took to the haymakers who gave her lots of hay in return. Rita gave the hay to the cow, who gave her a piece of butter. Rita ran quickly to Zippy, picked up the poor choking little thing and put some butter down her mouth. Zippy gave a little gasp, swallowed the bean and was quite better. And soon she was happily pecking about in the farm-yard with the rest of Rita's chicks.

Monkey see, Monkey do

————————— ✳ —————————

When Bimbo was a tiny baby monkey, he could not walk. He could not even crawl.

But he could cling to his mother's breast like this.

And that is the way Mother Monkey carried her baby about in the tree where they lived.

One day Bimbo's mother reached out for some fruit to eat.

Monkey see, Monkey do

Bimbo reached for fruit, too.

"Monkey see, Monkey do," said Mother. "You're too little to eat fruit. Babies drink milk."

Bimbo liked milk. He sucked up lots of milk from his mother's breast. And he grew bigger and bigger.

Then one day Mother said: "You're a big baby now. You will soon learn to crawl."

And baby Bimbo did learn to crawl. Sometimes he crawled out too far on a branch. Then his mother would reach out and pull him back. "Some branches are too small to hold you," she said. "Hop on my back, I'll show you."

Bimbo had a piggyback ride in the branches of the tree.

"You must test the branches to see if they'll hold you," said Mother Monkey.

Bimbo was having fun. He was learning to take care of himself too.

When he was a little older, Bimbo learned to climb. One day he climbed all the way up to the top of the tree.

Then he shouted: "Look at me. I climbed up to the top of the tree. See!"

"I see," chirped a little bird. "Now watch me."

The little bird spread his wings, hopped off the tree, and flew away. "I wish I could fly," thought Bimbo.

"I can cling. I can crawl and I can climb. Maybe I can fly too. I'll try."

So Bimbo waved his arms and jumped into the air.

But Bimbo didn't fly up.

He fell down—*Bump!*—to the ground.

"Ouch!" Bimbo began to scream.

Mother Monkey came running.

She picked up her little one in her arms.

"I tried to fly like the bird," cried Bimbo. "The bird flew away."

Monkey see, Monkey do

"Monkey see, Monkey do," said Mother. "That's silly. You are a monkey, not a bird.

"The bird has wings, and you do not have wings. You cannot fly, but there are many things that monkeys can do," said Mother. "You'll find out."

Then for a long time Bimbo had fun in the tree, finding out what he could do.

He could climb like this.

He could swing.

He could jump from tree to tree like this.

Bimbo was growing big and strong.

Every night Mother Monkey told her son stories about the jungle.

"The lion is the King of the Jungle," said Mother. "He roars so loud that the jungle shakes. All animals fear the lion.

"But we monkeys live in the treetops, and *here* we are safe.

"Always remember, Bimbo, when danger comes, climb a tree."

"I'm a big boy now," said Bimbo.

And he *was* quite a big boy. Sometimes he climbed down out of the tree and walked in the jungle. One day he saw a mole crawling along close to the ground.

"I can walk," said Bimbo. "I crawled when I was a baby, but now I can walk standing up. See!"

"I do not see," said the mole. "I do not need to see. I live underground." And he crawled into his hole.

Bimbo tried to crawl in after the mole, but he could only get his head in.

He was stuck, and he began to howl.

Mother Monkey heard and came running. She pulled Bimbo's head out of the hole.

"Monkey see, Monkey do, Monkey gets in trouble too," said Mother. "Your head is for thinking, Bimbo, not for sticking into holes."

Bimbo began to cry like a baby.

"Carry me home. Carry me home."

"You will have to ride on my back," said Mother. "I have a new baby now. She is your baby sister. See! She is riding on the underside."

"That's my place," screamed Bimbo.

"You're not a baby any more," said Mother. "If you want to ride, get on my back."

Bimbo climbed up on his mother's back. "Look!" he said, and began to laugh. "My baby sister is trying to climb up on your back, too."

"Monkey see, Monkey do," said Mother.

"That's baby stuff," said Bimbo. "I'm not a baby."

Monkey see, Monkey do

"Of course not," said Mother. "You can think for yourself and decide what to do."

"Sure I can," shouted Bimbo. And he jumped off his mother's back and walked off into the jungle all by himself.

He met an elephant carrying her baby with her trunk, like this.

"That's a funny way to carry a baby," said Bimbo.

"I like it," said the baby elephant.

"Babies need that," said Bimbo. "It looks like fun, but I'm not a baby any more. I don't need to be carried. I can walk by myself. I can climb too, and swing from tree to tree.

"And I can think of what to do. Can you?"

Monkey see, Monkey do

"He's learning," said Mother Elephant.

Bimbo walked along, feeling like a big boy. And he came to a river. There was a turtle on the river bank.

The turtle pulled his head and legs into his shell.

Bimbo knocked on the shell. "Come out, Turtle!" he said. "I won't hurt you."

"Better safe than sorry," said the turtle, sticking his head out. Then he slid into the water.

Bimbo was about to slide in the water too, but this time he stopped to think.

"Maybe I can't swim like a turtle."

"Oh, come on in," croaked a frog, and he jumped into the river.

"But you have webbed feet, and I have not," shouted Bimbo.

"*I* don't have webbed feet," said a big hippopotamus, rising out of the water, "and I live in the water."

"But I live in a tree," said Bimbo.

Then suddenly the turtle, the frog and the hippopotamus disappeared under water. And a terrible alligator came up out of the water, opened his great big, huge, enormous mouth and shouted: "Come on in, I love monkeys."

Bimbo was terrified. He was so scared he didn't know what to do.

WHAT WOULD YOU DO?

Well, Bimbo didn't do anything right away. But he thought about what to do, and he remembered that his mother had said: "When danger comes, climb a tree." So he ran all the way home and climbed his own tree, and there he found another monkey.

"Who are you?" said Bimbo.

"I'm Jocko," said the monkey.

"What are you doing in *my* tree?" said Bimbo.

"I was just swinging on a vine, and I landed here."

Monkey see, Monkey do

"Gee," said Bimbo. "Can you swing from tree to tree?"

"Of course," said Jocko. "I'll show you," and he swung out into the air and landed in his own tree.

Then Bimbo grabbed a long vine and swung over beside Jocko.

"Now you're in my tree."

"I'm sorry," said Bimbo. "I didn't stop to think. Let's be friends. We can have fun together.

"Let's swing back to my tree together.

"Now let's race down the tree."

"You won!" said Jocko.

"Well," said Bimbo as the two friends walked along together, "I *should* win. I was born in that tree. I played in the branches when I was little. Once I tried to fly like a bird."

"That was foolish," said Jocko.

"I know," said Bimbo. "My mother said, 'Monkey see, Monkey do'."

Jocko started to laugh, but he stopped suddenly when. . . .

An antelope leaped by, screaming, "Run for your life!"

Then came an ostrich, shouting "Danger, run, run!"

A big rhinoceros followed, bellowing.

Then came a hyena and a zebra, all screaming and running, one after the other.

Jocko followed along. So did Bimbo, but Bimbo was shouting: "Climb, Jocko! Climb a tree. This is no time for running. Let's climb."

So they climbed the nearest tree.

And they were sitting there, trembling and trying to think about what to do, when a giraffe stuck his head into the branches of the tree.

"How did you get up here?" asked Bimbo.

"I'm not up here," said the giraffe. "My feet are on the ground."

"Why aren't you running from danger like the other animals?" asked Jocko.

"Because those sillies are running away from nothing at all. One of them got scared and screamed. The rest just followed."

"Monkey see, Monkey do," said Bimbo. "I'm hungry. Let's go down to the river and eat."

"Slide down my neck," said the giraffe.

"Whoops! What fun," said Jocko.

"My turn," said Bimbo. "Whee-e-e!"

When Bimbo and Jocko came to the river, it was getting dark and they were a long way from home.

Then the lion roared.

Monkey see, Monkey do

All the jungle knew what that meant. The roar of the lion shook the jungle, and the animals trembled and ran this way and that.

Bimbo was scared stiff, but this time he didn't run. He knew just what to do.

WHAT DO YOU THINK HE DID?

He climbed a tree. The *nearest* tree, as fast as he could. And so did Jocko.

There were many monkeys in the tree, screaming with terror.

"Quiet!" shouted Bimbo. "The lion will hear you."

"Come on, Jocko," whispered Bimbo. "We will climb to the top of the tree and think about what to do."

"Hurry, Bimbo," said Jocko. "Hurry."

"I'm testing the branches," said Bimbo, "to see if they'll hold me. If a branch breaks, I'll fall to the ground. Then the big lion will surely eat me up."

"I wish I were home with my mother," said Jocko.

Bimbo looked down. The other monkeys were following him. "Stay where you are. *Please!*" he called. "The top-most branches will not hold all of us. Let us be still and think."

Monkey see, Monkey do

When they reached the treetop, the moon was bright.

"Here comes the King of Beasts," whispered Bimbo. "How noble he looks."

"He's so big and fierce," said Jocko, "but let's be quiet. If the monkeys down below know that the lion is here, some silly ones will start to scream, and the others will do the same."

"You are wise, my friend," said Bimbo. "We will wait until the lion has passed before we let them know."

Then suddenly in the still of the night a hyena laughed.

"That's a laughing hyena," said Bimbo. "He is waiting for the lion's kill. He will eat the bones. There goes the lion. He's after the hyena."

"Let's be sure he's gone before we tell the others," said Jocko.

So they waited. And when all was still in the jungle, Bimbo shouted to the monkeys below, "The lion has passed by this tree."

Then there was a scramble in the tree below. All those silly monkeys started to climb down out of the tree.

"Stop," shouted Bimbo. "Stop and think. The lion will prowl through the jungle all night, hunting for food.

"It will not be safe to leave the tree until morning. Then the lion will go back to his den and sleep all day."

"How do you know all these things?" asked Jocko.

"My mother taught me the ways of the jungle when I was a baby," said Bimbo.

"Now I have a baby sister. I can teach her. Look, its morning! Let's go. I'll show you my baby sister."

So Bimbo took his friend back to his tree, where they found Mother Monkey waiting.

And they told her all about what happened during the night.

"I'm proud of you, Bimbo," said Mother. "You used your head for thinking, not for sticking in a hole."

"Did he do that?" Jocko laughed.

Monkey see, Monkey do

"I did," said Bimbo, "when I was a baby. Where's my baby sister?"

"She's up in the tree," said Mother, "learning to climb, just as you did when you were a baby."

So Bimbo and Jock climbed up the tree.

AND WHAT DO YOU THINK THEY SAW?

Baby Sister was standing on a branch, watching a bird.

The bird spread his wings and hopped off.

Baby Sister waved her arms and was just about to jump when Bimbo grabbed her.

"Monkey see, Monkey do," said Bimbo.

Jocko laughed.

And Bimbo carried his baby sister back to her mother.

Pelle's New Clothes

---- ✱ ----

Young Pelle had a little lamb all his own and he himself saw to all its needs and wants. The little lamb grew bigger and bigger and so did Pelle. But as the lamb's wool grew longer and thicker, Pelle's suit grew smaller and smaller. So one day Pelle got hold of some shears and cut off all the lamb's wool. Then he put the wool into a bag and went to see his grandmother.

"Kind Grandmother," he said, "will you please card this wool for me?"

Pelle's New Clothes

"Of course I will, my dear," said his grandmother, and whilst I am doing it, be a good lad and dig up the weeds on my cabbage-patch."

So Pelle dug up the weeds and Grandmother carded Pelle's wool ever so carefully.

Then Pelle went to his other grandmother and said: "Kind Grandmother, will you please spin this wool into yarn for me?"

"Of course I will, my dear," said his grandmother, "and whilst I am doing it, be a good lad and keep an eye on my cows for me."

So Pelle looked after Grandmother's cows and Grandmother spun Pelle's wool ever so carefully.

Then Pelle went to see his uncle, the painter, and asked him for some paint to colour his yarn with.

"That *is* a funny notion," smiled his uncle. "I haven't got that sort of paint, you know. But I'll tell you what to do. Here's a pound. Go to that shop on the other side of the river and buy me a bottle of turpentine. Keep the change and buy yourself some dye with it. *That* is what you need to colour your yarn with."

"Thank you very much, Uncle," said Pelle. He took the pound, went to the riverside and rowed over to the shop, where he bought a bottle of turpentine for his uncle. Then in the same shop he bought a big bag of dye with the change.

Then he rowed back, took the dye home and dyed the wool all by himself until every bit of it was blue.

Then Pelle took the wool to his mother. "Please, Mother," he said, "will you weave this wool for me?"

"Of course I will, my dear," said his mother, "but whilst I am doing it, be a good lad and look after your little sister for me."

So Pelle looked after his little sister, and his mother wove the wool very carefully into cloth.

Then Pelle went to the tailor and asked him: "Please, Mr. Tailor, will you make a suit out of this cloth for me?"

"Of course, my little man," said the tailor, "but in return you must rake my hay, gather in the firewood and feed my pigs."

So Pelle went to work. He raked the tailor's hay, brought in his firewood and fed his pigs. The tailor was ever so pleased and he hurried to finish Pelle's suit so that it was all ready by Saturday evening.

And on Sunday morning Pelle put on his new suit and went to the lamb and said, "Thank you very much for this beautiful new suit."

And the lamb said: "Baa-a-a, baa-a-a," and it sounded very much as though the lamb was laughing with pleasure and was as pleased as Pelle himself—for it was out of his wool that Pelle had got his nice new suit.

Little Laura on the River

---- ✳ ----

The Big River ran through the Great City where little Laura lived. Little Laura loved to walk by the River, wearing her moufflon hat, with her best friend, Billie Guftie, and her beloved Nannie.

One day they went down to the Pier to watch the Pleasure Boats coming in. They saw the Gaiety Belle arrive.

"Can *we* go on a pleasure boat, Nannie?" asked Little Laura.

"Good gracious me!" cried Nannie.

"Oh, *please*, Nannie," said Billie Guftie. "We will be good."

"In that case we will go," said Nannie.

They hurried down the gangway to a pleasure boat, the Gaiety Belle. But as they approached she moved off.

"Full up! Full up!" cried those on board. "No room! No room!"

It was feared that this unfortunate turn of events might make Laura weep. But just then a small craft was seen speeding over the waters. As it approached they saw that it was the River Police Speed Boat ... and at the helm was none other than Grebo.

Grebo the Special. The Most Special of all Special Policemen. He who wore the Brass Badge of Justice and the Plumes of the Red Shrike. No one but Grebo might wear the Brass Badge of Justice and the Plumes of the Red Shrike.

"Will you come for a spin in the speed boat?" asked Grebo. Nannie declined this invitation.

"I am too fat for that little boat," she said. Nevertheless she allowed the children to go with Grebo, and sat herself down on a chair on the Pier to await their return.

"Take care of Laura, Billie Guftie," she called as she waved them "Good-bye."

So off they went, those fortunate children, up the River in the River Police Speed Boat with Grebo, the Special, the Most Special of all Special Policemen. Past many famous buildings and under bridges.

"On my left," said Grebo, "you see the King's Water Palace. And there is the Royal Boat House where the Royal Barge is kept."

They sped past the Gaiety Belle to the amazement and envy of those passengers.

"Oo Umph," the passengers cried, as the swell from the speed boat nearly unseated them.

But the speed boat dashed on . . . past factories and ware-

houses and cranes . . . till they got to the docks.

They saw the great liners and merchant ships.

"Ho, Ho!" said Grebo. "There's the S.S. QUEENIE, the largest liner in the world. Let us go and look at her."

Grebo pointed out to Billie Guftie the merits of this fine liner, but Laura was more interested in a swan.

As it glided by she slipped on the swan's back. "Ah, Ha! What larkish fun!" she cried.

But soon she was frightened as the bird glided swiftly, swiftly down the River away from Grebo and Billie Guftie.

"Help! Help!" she cried in terror, but her voice was lost on the waters.

The situation was getting very serious when the sound of music and laughter was heard. What was it?

It was the Royal Barge! In it were the King and his body-guard, Sir Archie Argyle. The King was sitting on a Nautical Throne which was decorated with shells and fishes made of gold.

Sir Archie was rowing. He complained that his arms were aching.

Little Laura on the River

"I am weary with rowing," he sighed.

"Then rest a while and I will sing for you," said the King. The swan floated close to the Royal Barge to listen to the song.

> "Oh! What a wondrous thing
> To be a Royal King,
> To laugh! To float! To sing!
> Ho! Ho! Ho! Ho!
> Ha! Ha! Ha! Ha!"

Suddenly the King saw Laura. "Hullo, dear child. What on earth are you doing there?"

The King invited her to sit with him on the Nautical Throne and Sir Archie lifted her on board. The swan glided gracefully away.

"I'm lost," said Laura.

"Then we will help you to get found," replied the King. "Row on, Argyle."

Laura enjoyed sitting on the Nautical Throne beside the King.

Meanwhile Grebo and Billie Guftie were anxiously scanning the waters. They were very worried.

"What will Nannie say?" thought Billie Guftie.

Imagine how delighted they were when the Royal Barge hoved into sight, with Laura sitting beside the King on the Nautical Throne!

"Ahoy there, Grebo!" called the King.

Grebo brought the Special Boat alongside the Royal Barge. They were all thankful to see each other.

"What fun it must be to travel at such a speed as you do, Grebo," said the King. "I would love to travel at such a pace. This barge goes *so* slowly."

Grebo offered to tie the Speed Boat to the Royal Barge. "What a marvellous idea," cried the King. "He is going to tow us."

Off they went! "Faster! Faster!" cried the King as Grebo flogged the Speed Boat through the waters.

Once more they speeded past the Gaiety Belle.

"There's Nannie! There's Nannie!" cried Little Laura.

Nannie loved Royalty so she was very excited when the Royal Barge came into view. Imagine her astonishment when she saw Laura sitting beside the King on the Nautical Throne.

"Back again safe and sound," said the King as they came to the Pier.

"Your Majesty! Your Majesty!" sighed Nannie as she curtsied low.

As the children scrambled on to the Pier the Great Clock struck.

ONE . . . TWO . . . THREE . . . FOUR . . . FIVE.

"Tea time," said little Laura, "I'd like to go home now."

"And I must go home to my Water Palace," said the King. "What fun we have all had to-day. Goodbye my friends, goodbye."

They waved and waved until the Royal Barge had disappeared from view.

Mrs. Pepperpot and the Mechanical Doll

— ✳ —

It was two days before Christmas. Mrs. Pepperpot hummed and sang as she trotted round her kitchen, she was so pleased to be finished with all her Christmas preparations. The pig had been killed, the sausages made, and now all she had to do was to brew herself a cup of coffee and sit down for a little rest.

"How lovely that Christmas is here," she said, "then everybody's happy—especially the children—that's the best of all; to see them happy and well."

The old woman was almost like a child herself because of this knack she had of suddenly shrinking to the size of a pepperpot.

She was thinking about all this while she was making her coffee, and she had just poured it into the cup when there was a knock at the door.

"Come in," she said, and in came a little girl who was oh! so pale and thin.

"Poor child! Wherever do you live—I'm sure I've never seen you before," said Mrs. Pepperpot.

"I'm Hannah. I live in the little cottage at the edge of the forest," said the child, "and I'm just going round to all the houses to ask if anybody has any old Christmas decorations left over from last year—glitter or paper-chains or glass balls or anything, you know. Have *you* got anything you don't need?"

"I expect so, Hannah," answered Mrs. Pepperpot, and went up into the attic to fetch the cardboard box with all the decorations. She gave it to the little girl.

"How lovely! Can I really have all that?"

"You can," said Mrs. Pepperpot, "and you shall have something else as well. Tomorrow I will bring you a big doll."

"I don't believe that," said Hannah.

"Why not?"

"You haven't *got* a doll."

"That's simple; I'll buy one," said Mrs. Pepperpot. "I'll bring it over tomorrow afternoon, but I must be home by six o'clock because it's Christmas Eve."

"How wonderful if you can come tomorrow afternoon—I shall be all alone. Father and Mother both go out to work, you see, and they don't get back until the church bells have rung."

Mrs. Pepperpot and the Mechanical Doll

So the little girl went home, and Mrs. Pepperpot went down to the toy-shop and bought a big doll. But when she woke up next morning there she was, once more, no bigger than a pepperpot.

"How provoking!" she said to herself. "On this day of all days, when I have to take the doll to Hannah. Never mind! I expect I'll manage."

After she had dressed she tried to pick up the doll, but it was much too heavy for her to lift.

"I'll have to go without it," she thought, and opened the door to set off.

But oh dear! it had been snowing hard all night, and the little old woman soon sank deep in the snowdrifts. The cat was sitting in front of the house; when she saw something moving in the snow she thought it was a mouse and jumped on it.

"Hi, stop!" shouted Mrs. Pepperpot. "Keep your claws to yourself! Can't you see it's just me, shrunk again?"

"I beg your pardon," said the cat, and started walking away.

"Wait a minute," said Mrs. Pepperpot, "to make up for your mistake you can give me a ride down to the main road." The cat was quite willing, so she lay down and let the little old woman climb on her back. When they got to the main road the cat stopped. "Can you hear anything?" asked Mrs. Pepperpot.

"Yes, I think it's the snow-plough," said the cat, "so we'll have to get out of the way, or we'll be buried in snow."

"I don't want to get out of the way," said Mrs. Pepperpot, and she sat down in the middle of the road and waited till the snow-plough was right in front of her; then she jumped up and landed smack on the front tip of the plough.

There she sat, clinging on for dear life and enjoying herself hugely. "Look at me, the little old woman, driving the snow-plough!" she laughed.

When the snow-plough had almost reached the door of

Hannah's little cottage, she climbed on to the edge nearest the side of the road and, before you could say Jack Robinson, she had landed safely on the great mound of snow thrown up by the plough. From there she could walk right across Hannah's hedge and slide down the other side. She was shaking the snow off her clothes on the doorstep when Hannah came out and picked her up.

"Are you one of those mechanical dolls that you wind up?" asked Hannah.

"No," said Mrs. Pepperpot, "I am a woman who can wind myself up, thank you very much. Help me brush off all the snow and then let's go inside."

Mrs. Pepperpot and the Mechanical Doll

"Are you perhaps the old woman who shrinks to the size of a pepperpot?"

"Of course I am, silly."

"Where's the doll you were going to bring me?" asked Hannah when they got inside.

"I've got it at home. You'll have to go back with me and fetch it. It's too heavy for me!

"Shouldn't you have something to eat, now that you've come to see me? Would you like a biscuit?" And the little girl held out a biscuit in the shape of a ring.

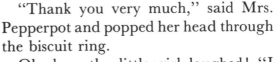

"Thank you very much," said Mrs. Pepperpot and popped her head through the biscuit ring.

Oh, how the little girl laughed! "I quite forgot you were so small," she said; "let me break it into little pieces so that you can eat it." Then she fetched a thimble and filled it with fruit juice. "Have a drink," she said.

"Thank you," said Mrs. Pepperpot.

After that they played a lot of good games; ride-a-cock-horse with Mrs. Pepperpot sitting on Hannah's knee, and hide-and-seek. But the little girl had an awful time trying to find Mrs. Pepperpot—she hid in such awkward places. When they had finished playing Hannah put on her coat and with Mrs. Pepperpot in her pocket she went off to fetch her beautiful big doll.

"Oh, thank you!" she exclaimed when she saw it. "But do you know," she added, "I would really rather have *you* to play with all the time."

"You can come and see me again if you like," said Mrs.

Mrs. Pepperpot and the Mechanical Doll

Pepperpot. "I am often as small as a pepperpot, and then it's nice to have a little help around the house. And, of course, we can play games as well."

So now the little girl often spends her time with Mrs. Pepperpot. She looks ever so much better, and they often talk about the day Mrs. Pepperpot arrived on the snow-plough, and about the doll she gave Hannah.

A Growing Tale

---------------------------- * ----------------------------

There was once a boy called Tim.

He was smaller than his sister Sally and smaller than his brother Billy. He was the smallest person in the house, except the kitten and the canary, and you can't count them.

Tim was so tiny he could only just walk, he could only just talk and he only had one candle on his birthday cake. So you can guess how small he was.

He couldn't wash himself, he couldn't dress himself, and he couldn't blow his own nose. His mother had to do almost everything for him. She gave him a tiny chair to sit on, and a tiny bed to sleep in every night.

A Growing Tale

He didn't know his right foot from his left foot. He didn't know what was red and what was blue. He couldn't say what one and one makes. He was much too small to count.

He was very good at shouting, at banging and at bawling. He was very good at throwing, at grabbing and at crawling. Tim was so very tiny he could walk beneath the table and never bump his head!

But he wished and he wished he could see over fences, and turn door handles all by himself.

He grew and he grew until he was two, he grew and he grew until he was three, and he grew and he grew and then was FOUR. And when he was four, Tim was a Great Big Boy. He had four candles on his birthday cake.

He could see over fences and what was on tables. He could now turn door handles, all by himself.

He was MUCH too big for his tiny little chair, he was much too big for his tiny little cot, so he slept in a real bed of his very own. He could wash himself, dress himself, and blow his nose on a great big pocket handkerchief. He put his left shoe on his left foot, his right shoe on his right foot, and he tied both the laces in a very tidy bow. He knew what was red and what was blue, so he didn't bother bawling and he didn't bother crawling. He was much too big for that!

Tim was now so BIG, he went to the Nursery School. What do you think of that?

He was still much smaller than his sister Sally, and he was still much smaller than his big brother Billy. For they had grown too!

The Little Armchair

————————————— * —————————————

In the sitting-room there were six armchairs. There was the Very Big Chair where Father always sat. It was tall and wide and had fat arms, and although perhaps it was getting a little shabby it was the most comfortable chair you could imagine. Father loved it dearly.

"What he would do without me I cannot think," the Very Big Chair told the others. "Do you know the moment I like best in the day?"

"No," said Mother's Chair. "Tell us!"

"It is the moment when Father sits down in me in the evening after he has had a very busy day. He stretches out his long legs to the fire and he gives a long, happy sigh. 'Ah-a-a-ah!' he says, 'It's good to be home again'."

Mother's Chair smiled. She was smaller and prettier and she lived on the other side of the fireplace. "I too am very comfortable," she said. "When Mother has finished cooking and washing up and all the other things she is always busy doing, she loves to sit in me and listen to the radio or read. I like that. She treats me so kindly. Never thinks of dropping cigarette ash on my arms!"

"I *like* cigarette ash," said the Very Big Chair. "I like the smell."

"That is just as well," laughed the Rocking Chair, which

stood beside him. "Plenty of it falls on you. Now I would rather be myself than either of you."

"And why is that?" asked Mother's Chair.

"Oh, there are lots of reasons. For one thing, I am the only chair in the room which can rock."

"Ah, but you can't rock by yourself," objected the Very Big Chair.

"I don't wish to rock by myself. I like Granny to come and sit in me. Then, backwards and forwards, backwards and forwards we go. See-saw, see-saw. Oh, it's a lovely feeling!"

The two Visitors' Chairs, which stood a little farther away, nodded to one another as if to say: "Yes, yes, it must be lovely to rock."

They never joined in the conversation very much because they hardly seemed part of the family. They looked quite handsome and they were very comfortable, but almost always it was people who did not live in the house who sat in them.

The Rocking Chair was still talking away to herself, her voice growing quieter and quieter. "Sometimes," she was saying, "Granny puts down her knitting and her eyes close. She dreams of days long ago, when she was a girl, and I begin to dream too. I dream of all the people who have sat in me, who have sat . . . sat . . . in . . ." The Rocking Chair did not finish what she was going to say because she had fallen fast asleep. She often did that.

"Oh dear!" said Mother's Chair. "She has dropped off to sleep again. But then, of course, she is getting very old, you know."

All this time the Little Armchair, which lived on the other side of the room, had said nothing at all. She was so small that the others often forgot that she was there. Nobody ever sat in her. She used to wish so much that somebody tiny would come to the house so that she might be used. Sometimes she heard the other chairs whispering to each other. One of them would say: "I

can't think why the Little Armchair is here at all. She is much
too small for anyone to use."

And one of the others would answer: "I quite agree. Why
don't they take her away to another part of the house? She is
only in the way. Then there would be more room for the rest
of us."

All this made the Little Armchair sad. But one day she heard
something which made her feel a little happier. Mother and
Father were talking about some friends who were coming to
stay with them. They mentioned two grown-ups and somebody
they called "the little one".

When the fire had died down and the family had gone up-
stairs to bed, the chairs talked about this news they had over-
heard.

"The grown-ups who are coming to stay will sit in us, of

course," said a Visitor's Chair. "That will make a pleasant change."

"It will, indeed," said her friend. "And, perhaps," he turned to the Little Armchair, "perhaps 'the little one' might sit in you."

They were all very curious to see what would happen and the Little Armchair became quite excited. But the day before the visitors were to arrive the door opened and Father and Mother carried in a very strange thing. It was a high chair, made of wood, with a little tray in front of it.

"There!" said Mother, happily. "That will do splendidly for the baby."

The Little Armchair's heart sank. The baby! So "the little one" was a baby! This meant that she would not be used after all. That night she heard the Very Big Chair tell the others that it would really be very much better if the Little Armchair were taken away, for she was of no use at all. With all these new people coming the room would be much too crowded. This made her feel very miserable and she creaked and sighed all by herself on the other side of the room.

The next day the visitors arrived. There were two grown-ups, there was a baby, and . . . and . . . The Little Armchair's heart almost stopped beating. Coming through the door was a small girl, who was perhaps about five years old. She was holding her father's hand and she looked rather shy and serious. Suddenly, her little face broke into smiles. Her eyes shone and she ran straight across the room to the Little Armchair, crying: "Oh, the dear little chair! Oh, look at it! It was meant for me." After stroking its arms and dancing round and round, she sat down so that everyone could see how perfectly she fitted it.

The Little Armchair creaked with happiness. Somebody needed her. At last she felt part of the family. All the time the friends stayed in the house the small girl sat in her own little chair. Sometimes she sat looking at her picture books, sometimes she sat nursing her doll or her Teddy Bear, sometimes she knelt on the floor and used the seat of the Little Armchair as a table for her drawing book. And sometimes she simply sat with her hands on the arms and her small head resting on the cushion at the back, telling everyone that this was the most comfortable chair in the world.

But the day came at last when she had to go back to her own home. While the rest of the family were busy saying goodbye, she crept into the sitting-room and, kneeling on the floor, she laid her head on the seat of the Little Armchair.

"Dear little chair!" she whispered. "Goodbye, until I come again. It won't be long. Quite soon I shall come again."

Then she was gone. Yet the Little Armchair was not sad. Other visitors came to sit in the Visitors' Chairs; Father sat

smoking in the Very Big Chair, Mother sat reading in *her* chair; Granny knitted and dreamed in the Rocking Chair. The Little Armchair, who used to be lonely, did not feel now that nobody wanted her. Happily and patiently she waited, for she knew that one day quite soon the small girl would come back again. Each morning she said to herself: "Who knows? It might even be today."

Big Sister and Little Sister

———————————— * ————————————

O nce there was a big sister and a little sister. The big sister always took care. Even when she was skipping, she took care that her little sister stayed on the path. When she rode her bicycle, she gave her little sister a ride. When she was walking to school, she took the little sister's hand and helped her cross the road. When they were playing in the fields, she made sure little sister didn't get lost. When they were sewing, she made sure little sister's needle was threaded and that little sister held the scissors the right way. Big sister took care of everything, and little sister thought there was nothing big sister couldn't do. Little sister would sometimes cry, but big sister always made her stop. First she'd put her arm around her, then she'd hold out her handkerchief and say, "Here, blow." Big sister knew everything.

Big Sister and Little Sister

"Don't do it like that," she'd say.

"Do it this way."

And little sister did. Nothing could bother big sister. She knew too much.

But one day little sister wanted to be alone. She was tired of big sister saying,

"Sit here."

"Go there."

"Do it this way."

"Come along."

And while big sister was getting lemonade and biscuits for them, little sister slipped away, out of the house, out of the garden, down the road, and into the meadow where daisies and grass hid her. Very soon she heard big sister calling, calling, and calling her. But she didn't answer. She heard big sister's voice getting louder when she was close and fainter when she went the other way, calling, calling. Little sister leaned back in the daisies. She thought about lemonade and biscuits. She thought about the book big sister had promised to read to her. She thought about big sister saying,

"Sit here."

"Go there."

"Do it this way."

"Come along."

No one told little sister anything now. The daisies bent back and forth in the sun. A big bee bumbled by. The weeds scratched under her bare legs. But she didn't move. She heard big sister's voice coming back. It came closer and closer and closer. And suddenly big sister was so near little sister could have touched her. But big sister sat down in the daisies. She stopped calling. And she began to cry. She cried and cried just the way little sister often did. When the little sister cried, the big one comforted her. But there was no one to put an arm around big

sister. No one took out a handkerchief and said, "Here, blow,"
Big sister just sat there crying alone.

Little sister stood up but big sister didn't even see her, she
was crying so much. Little sister went over and put her arm
around big sister. She took out her handkerchief and said
kindly, "Here, blow." Big sister did. Then the little sister
hugged her.

"Where have you been?" big sister asked.

"Never mind," said little sister. "Let's go home and have some lemonade."

And from that day on little sister and big sister both took care of each other because little sister had learned from big sister and now they both knew how.